Black Refugees in Canada

Black Refugees in Canada

Accounts of Escape During the Era of Slavery

GEORGE HENDRICK AND
WILLENE HENDRICK

McFarland & Company, Inc., Publishers
Jefferson, North Carolina, and London

Frontispiece: Escaping slaves were in danger from search parties, bloodhounds, bounty hunters, and wild animals (University of Illinois at Urbana-Champaign Library).

LIBRARY OF CONGRESS CATALOGUING-IN-PUBLICATION DATA

Hendrick, George.
　　Black refugees in Canada : accounts of escape during the era of slavery / by George Hendrick and Willene Hendrick.
　　　　p.　　cm.
　　Includes bibliographical references and index.

　　ISBN 978-0-7864-4733-6
　　softcover : 50# alkaline paper ∞

　　1. Fugitive slaves—United States—Biography.　2. Fugitive slaves—Canada—Biography.　3. Slaves—United States—Social conditions.　4. African Americans—Canada—Biography. 5. Blacks—Canada—Biography.　[1. Underground Railroad—Canada.]　I. Hendrick, Willene, 1928–　II. Title.
　　E450.H515　2010
　　971'.00496—dc22　　　　　　　　　　　　　　　　2010002294

British Library cataloguing data are available

©2010 George Hendrick and Willene Hendrick. All rights reserved

No part of this book may be reproduced or transmitted in any form or by any means, electronic or mechanical, including photocopying or recording, or by any information storage and retrieval system, without permission in writing from the publisher.

Cover images ©2010 Clipart.com and ©2010 Photos.com

Manufactured in the United States of America

McFarland & Company, Inc., Publishers
　Box 611, Jefferson, North Carolina 28640
　　www.mcfarlandpub.com

For
Ray Elliott, George Fortenberry, Paul Friedman,
R. Baird Shuman, Jean Thompson, and Emily Watts,
our friends for many years.
And for our grandchildren, Emilie and Dennis,
who like to have books dedicated to them.

Acknowledgments

Librarians at the Urbana Free Library and the University of Illinois at Urbana-Champaign helped us locate materials, and the Urbana Free Library reference staff provided us with many inter-library loan items. Robert Shaddy, Special and Area Studies Department, University of Florida Library, provided us with illustrations from *The Young People's Illustrated Edition of "Uncle Tom's" Story of His Life*. The Archives of Ontario, Buxton National Site & Museum, University of Illinois at Urbana-Champaign Library, and Uncle Tom's Cabin Museum provided us with images. Sarah Hendrick Jourdain undertook computer searches for us and helped with the gathering of illustrations.

Table of Contents

Acknowledgments   vii
Preface   1

1. Blacks in Canada: The Early Years   3
2. Shadrach   19
3. Josiah Henson and Eliza Harris   23
4. Madison Washington   54
5. The Shadd Family   59
6. Lewis Richardson, Formerly a Slave on Henry Clay's Plantation   73
7. The Blackburns   77
8. Ann Maria Jackson   84
9. Harriet Tubman   88
10. John Fairfield, Southern Abolitionist Who Helped Slaves Escape to Canada   92
11. Chaplain Garland H. White   97
12. Dr. A.T. Augusta   107
13. The Abbott Family   110
14. John Henry Hill   113
15. Mr. and Mrs. John Little   119

Table of Contents

16. Narratives by Refugees in Three Canadian Towns: An Except from *The Refugees: A North-Side View of Slavery* (1856)   130
17. Statements By and About Black Refugees in Canada   157
18. God Save Queen Victoria   163

Chapter Notes   167
Bibliography   175
Index   179

Preface

"No more auction block for me, No more, no more, No more auction block for me, Many thousand gone," they sang. Many thousand also sang, "I ain't got long to stay here."[1] Thousands of black people sought refuge in Canada before the Civil War, and we tell the stories of these refugees: why they decided to escape slavery, how they made it to Canada, what their lives were like in this new country. Several risked capture by returning to try to recover family members still in servitude. After the end of the Civil War, large numbers of blacks left Canada, hoping for a better life in the United States after slavery had been abolished.

In telling these stories of black people, we have used slave narratives and nineteenth-century interviews from four main sources— Benjamin Drew's *The Refugee: A North-Side View of Slavery*, S.G. Howe's *The Refugees from Slavery in Canada West*, the more complete Howe interviews in John Blassingame's *Slave Testimony*, and William Still's *The Underground Rail-Road*— as well as scholarly and proper studies, especially Robin Winks's *The Blacks in Canada*, Daniel G. Hill's *The Freedom-Seekers: Blacks in Early Canada*, Karolyn Smardz Frost's *I've Got a Home in Glory Land: A Lost Tale of the Underground Railroad*, Wilbur H. Siebert's *The Underground Railroad from Slavery to Freedom*, Jaqueline L. Tobin's *From Midnight to Dawn: The Last Tracks of the Underground Railroad*, Fergus M. Bordewich's *Bound for Canaan: The Underground Railroad and the War for the Soul of America*, Ann Hagedorn's *Beyond the River: The Untold Story of the Underground Railroad*, Adam Hochschild's *Bury the Chains: Prophets and Rebels in the Fight to Free an Empire's Slaves*, and Simon Schama's *Rough Crossings: Britain, the Slaves and the American Revolution*.

Preface

Most of the materials we used refer to fugitives in Canada West, now Ontario.

To provide a context for these stories, we have also included a short account of slavery in Canada before it was abolished in 1833 by Parliament in London. We include brief accounts of various colonies for blacks in this northern country, although these colonies were most often failures. We do not minimize the racism of whites in Canada and the discrimination many blacks felt in their new country. It must be admitted too that the accounts of black life and experience from this period reflect the biases of the narrators. Blacks who were interviewed in Canada had their own agendas when they told their stories, and the editors, reporters, and interviewers also certainly shaped the stories and events they chronicled.

We have retold a long interesting account about a white slave-stealer titled "John Fairfield, Southern Abolitionist Who Helped Slaves Escape to Canada," by Levi Coffin, friend of escaping slaves.

Blacks in slavery were denied formal schooling, but some did learn to read and write. We quote several of their letters written after they reached Canada; the spelling is often phonetic. We have not corrected the spelling and have not used *sic* to indicate the spelling is incorrect. Non-standard punctuation in letters and quotations is also unchanged.

We also include philosophical musings of refugees on their lives in the United States and Canada. As Mrs. Isaac Riley, who escaped from slavery in Perry County, Missouri, to Buxton in Canada West, observed: "I think my present condition here is preferable to what it would have been in slavery. There we were in darkness, — here we are in light. My children also would have grown up, had I remained there, in ignorance and darkness."[2]

1

Blacks in Canada
The Early Years[1]

In 1629 the Englishman David Kirke, a privateer, captured Quebec City and that same year he sold for 50 half-crowns a black child, probably six years old, brought to the New World directly from Madagascar. The purchaser was a French clerk, who then sold the little boy to Guillaume Couillard. Quebec City did not remain under British control long and was returned to France in 1632. The child received religious instruction and was baptized in 1633; he was then given the name Olivier LeJeune. Olivier was undoubtedly not the first slave in French Canada, but little is known about the earlier ones—their names are unknown, and they now seem to be untraceable. Much of Olivier's history is also lost, but his owner obviously needed domestic help; Couillard had ten children and 100 acres of land, 20 of which were in cultivation, and he had plans to open a flour mill. Couillard may have been a benevolent master, but it is likely that as a child and young man Olivier LeJeune had a hard life. He would have been working on the farm, helping with the crops and caring for farm animals, and at the same time looking after children and working at the mill. He was apparently not completely docile, for in 1638 he was charged with slandering a settler and was put in chains for a day. He may well have been freed before his death in 1654, when he was about 30 years old. At that time he was described as a *domestique*.[2]

After three decades of misrule, the Company of New France gave up the charter it had held since France regained Quebec. In 1663 King Louis XIV moved to strengthen this colony: He appointed a governor, and there was a concerted effort to increase agriculture, mining, and fishing. By 1688, when there were about 9,000 people living in New France, there was a labor shortage, and Louis XIV was asked for permission to import slaves. On May 1, 1689, the King responded, giving limited approval: "His Majesty finds it good that the inhabitants of Canada import negroes to take care of their agriculture," but he warned that the cold climate might be a hazard for the slaves, bringing about their premature dimise.[3] Concerns about slaves from a warm climate in cold Canada were a recurring theme, but Africans who were well-clothed, housed and fed adapted well to the new environment. Most of the problems arose because the clothing, shelter, and diet were inadequate.

In addition to using Africans, colonists in Canada also enslaved *Panis* (Indians) for domestic, agricultural, and mining work. These Native Americans, though, had a way of melting into the bush and refusing to remain enslaved.

New work for African-born slaves developed after 1701 when Antoine de la Mothe Cadillac, from a minor aristocratic family, established a fur trading outpost on the Detroit River. French gentlemen in the group were unwilling to do the hard work necessary for success on the frontier, and at first they attempted to use captured *Panis*, who turned out to be absolutely uncooperative. The fur traders then brought in enslaved Africans to perform most of the manual labor.[4]

In 1709 Louis XIV gave permission for the New France colonists to own the slaves that they had already been allowed to import. The slavery system was part of the fabric of New France life. The Church did not oppose this slavery: Jesuits, Dominicans, and Franciscans all owned slaves. Government officials, the gentry, merchants, doctors, lawyers, and military officers owned slaves who were servants, farm workers, miners, and fishermen. It is not known precisely how many slaves there were in New France in the 18th century, but it has been proposed that in 1759 the number was 4,000 with 1,100 Africans and the rest *Panis*. The average age for the death of *Panis* was 17.7 and for blacks 25.2. *Panis* often died from diseases such as smallpox, but mistreatment and lack of clothing, food, and shelter undoubtedly played a part in the short life of all slaves.[5]

In 1760, after a long series of wars and skirmishes, British forces

1. Blacks in Canada

conquered New France, and in the peace treaty of 1763 the French ceded to their ancient enemy all of their North American possessions except for the vast Louisiana territory. The British, with their history as leaders in the profitable international slave trade and as users of slaves in their colonial territories, did not wish to interfere with slavery in their new possessions. British General Jeffrey Amherst assured the last of New France's governors: "Negroes and panis of both sexes shall remain in their quality of slaves in the possession of the French or Canadians to whom they belong; they shall be at liberty to keep them in the colony or sell them...." This assurance was included in the Articles of Capitulation as the British took control of a vast new territory.[6]

In the new British-controlled country, high government officials, the clergy, military officers, professional people, merchants, and farmers all owned slaves. These owners and most of the English and French speaking Canadians were, not surprisingly, prejudiced against blacks and accordingly believed in white supremacy.

The number in whites and blacks in Canada increased dramatically during and immediately after the Revolutionary War (1775–1783). British Loyalists fled the Thirteen Colonies, often taking their slaves with them, and settled in the Maritime Provinces and in Quebec. In the confusion of war, thousands of slaves in the Colonies escaped, some making their way to Canada. Additionally, a significant number of slaves gained freedom by joining British forces. On November 7, 1775, Lord Dunmore, British governor of Virginia, proclaimed: "I do hereby ... declare all indentured Servants, Negroes, or others (appertaining to Rebels,) free that are able and willing to bear Arms, they joining His Majesty's Troops, as soon as may be, for the more speedily reducing this Colony of a proper Sense of their Duty, to His Majesty's Crown and Dignity."[7]

While the Thirteen Colonies were not smashed into a state of the "proper Sense of their Duty," some slaves, after joining British troops, were later freed, uniting with other blacks who had run away. Others were still enslaved and owned by white Loyalists. About 500 blacks received land grants in Nova Scotia alone, but the parcels of government land were too small and the soil often rocky and poor. The blacks were frequently segregated, and they often suffered significant discrimination. Those blacks who were settled on more fertile land were more successful, but the Maritime Provinces were hardly a paradise for people of color.[8] Simon Schama, in *Rough Crossings: Britain, the Slaves and the American Revolution*, has a revealing account of the difficulties these blacks faced.

Several events in Britain had a profound effect on Slavery in Canada. James Somerset, a slave in Virginia, had been brought to England by his owner, Charles Stewart. Somerset escaped in 1771, was captured, and was to be sent to Jamaica. Somerset's plea for freedom came before the Court of King's Bench, presided over by Lord Mansfield, the Lord Chief Justice. Lord Mansfield was conservative by nature and could be expected to rule in favor of property rights. He was, though, troubled about returning a man to slavery and made many efforts to achieve an out-of-court settlement, which would have set Somerset free.[9]

Part of Lord Mansfield's dilemma about slavery can be traced to his own household. The Mansfields raised from infancy Dido Elizabeth Lindsay, the illegitimate daughter of his nephew who was an officer in the navy. Dido's mother was a slave on a ship the nephew had captured. Dido was an accepted member of the Mansfield family, and she received considerable funds from Lord Mansfield's estate after his death.

When all the efforts to settle the Somerset case out-of-court failed, on June 22, 1772, Lord Mansfield decided, as he later stated, that "The Master had no right to compel a slave to go into a foreign country."[10] Somerset was discharged, but Mansfield's ruling was narrowly focused and did not automatically free the other black slaves in the British Isles.

As Adam Hochschild showed in his recent book *Bury the Chains*, "Almost everyone believed that Mansfield had indeed outlawed slavery in England, including many lower-court judges who subsequently ruled against more than a dozen masters trying to assert ownership over slaves on English soil."[11] The misunderstood and misinterpreted ruling did encourage the anti-slavery movement throughout the British territories. The anti-slavery movement was especially supported by the Society of Friends (Quakers), a dissenting religious group with little

1. Blacks in Canada

political power. They were barred from serving in the House of Commons. The misinterpretation of the ruling in *Stewart vs. Somerset* also spread through the colonies.[12] There were always a few conscientious people who opposed slavery, usually on religious grounds.

A decade after the Mansfield ruling, a case of horror concerning slaves took place at sea. In 1783 the slave ship *Zong* sailed from the coast of Africa for Jamaica carrying 440 slaves. As was often the case on these crowded slave ships, diseases were endemic and large numbers of Africans began to die. Envisioning financial loss, the captain decided to throw all the sickest slaves overboard, some still shackled. He then planned to claim that their deaths were caused by "Perils ... of the seas," and then collect the £30 insurance which had been taken out on each of them. Just over 130 Africans were tossed overboard. The insurance company refused to pay, and the *Zong* owners then appealed, and that case was heard with Chief Justice Mansfield presiding. His lordship reverted to his natural inclination to protect property rights, remarking it was "just as if horses were killed." The court ruled that the case did not involve murder, since slaves were property, but "there appears to have been no necessity" to have thrown the slaves overboard.[13]

Seven years after the British government outlawed slavery throughout its territories, J.M.W. Turner painted "Slave Ship," which showed slaves that had been thrown overboard, their hands and arms still shackled. The violence of this horrific scene is emphasized by the red sky and the agitated sea. Some viewers of the painting in the 1840s would have remembered the story of the slaves thrown from the *Zong*. Most viewers then and now would be impressed and appalled by the brutality of the slave trade. Turner depicts "British crime on a vast scale,"[14] but he also indicts the French, Spanish, Portuguese, and American slave trade. Turner's painting does not show the name of the ship, nor the flag she was flying. Certainly other slave captains jettisoned African captives to the sharks. Turner's painting reminds viewers of the brutality and cruelty aboard every slave ship.

Several clergymen in England took up the *Zong* matter, and the story was certainly known in the British Isles and in the colonies and was used by the small band of abolitionists as they made their arguments against the immensely profitable slave trade.

In 1785, two years after the *Zong* scandal, Thomas Clarkson, a divinity student at Cambridge, won first prize for his Latin essay, "Is it lawful to make slaves of others against their will?"[15] The topic had been set by the Rev. Peter Peckard, vice-chancellor of the university, who knew about the despicable murders on the *Zong*. Clarkson was able to interview several people who had seen slavery up close, and he came to the unshakable belief that slavery was wrong. Clarkson won the prestigious prize, and later that year, having graduated from the university, he proceeded to London, where he translated his essay into English, expanding it with additional material.

Clarkson began to explore the possibility of publishing his work, and with a Quaker friend of his family called on the printer and bookseller James Phillips, who often did printing for Quakers. That day Clarkson decided that Phillips could print his manuscript. He began to learn more about the abolitionist activities of Quakers, and he soon met other Friends and heard the stories they had collected about the atrocities of slavery and about their own abolitionist efforts, which were often thwarted because they were seen as a "fringe" organization.

On the afternoon of May 22, 1787, nine Quakers and three Anglicans—all men—met at the Phillips shop to establish a committee to oppose slavery. The wealthy Quakers provided funds but had to work behind the scenes: The three Church of England members were the outside men who could present the case against slavery to the public and to government officials. Clarkson became the collector and disseminator of facts about slavery, riding on his horse to various port cities to interview ship captains and sailors connected with the slave trade and writing and publishing accounts of the British involvement in the slave trade.

As a tactic, the newly-formed committee worked first to abolish the slave trade itself. They began a well-designed plan of agitation, publishing pamphlets, approaching prominent people, preparing petitions, and making speaking tours.[16] In 1787, in a brilliant move, Clarkson approached William Wilberforce, a young, wealthy member of Parliament, who agreed to bring up the matter of slavery in the House of Commons. Wilberforce was also an Anglican, a requirement for serving in that body. He was a powerful speaker but a rather weak par-

1. Blacks in Canada

liamentarian, trying to see good in everyone and refraining from making sharp attacks on the merchants dealing in sugar and rum, the planters in the Caribbean, and the shipping interests, all of whom supported slavery.

Clarkson busied himself preparing materials to be used in parliamentary debates, but Wilberforce did not speak about the evils of slavery in the House of Commons until May 12, 1789. Parliamentary hearings then lasted until 1791. The committee of 12 had agitated brilliantly, gaining quick support for the cause with promotions not then in practice: they made large mailings of anti-slavery materials, gave out lapel pins, and began a boycott of slave-produced sugar. At least 300,000 Britons were engaged in the boycott.

The abolitionists submitted hundreds of pages of damaging testimony about the slave trade. The actual debate did not begin until April 18, 1791. Whatever chances there were to end the slave trade were stopped by a slave revolt in Dominica, which was soon blamed on the abolitionists. The House of Commons voted after two days of debate, 163 to 88, against the efforts to end the slave trade. Wilberforce and others went on agitating for parliament to take action, and they were finally successful in banning the slave trade in 1807. The efforts then shifted to ending slavery in all the British colonies, and a bill doing that finally passed in 1833, just weeks after the death of Wilberforce. Hochschild in *Bury the Chains* provides a brilliant account of that anti-slavery campaign.[17]

One of the young members of the House of Commons who supported Wilberforce in 1791 was John Graves Simcoe (1752–1806), son of a naval captain. He attended Eton, then Merton College, Oxford, but left before taking his degree to become an Ensign in the British army. He was sent to New England after the Revolutionary War began and served with distinction, rising to the rank of Lt. Colonel. As a military man, he realized that black people could help the war effort, and he proposed to enlist and lead Boston blacks in a British army unit, but his proposal was rejected. At the end of hostilities he returned to England, married an heiress, acquired an estate, and built a mansion, Wolford Lodge. He was elected to parliament from St. Maw's and took his seat on November 25, 1790. An Anglican, he spoke against slavery as being contrary to Christianity, and he argued that the unwritten British constitution did not expressly allow slavery.[18]

Simcoe did not stay in the House of Commons to fight the extended battles to end slavery. Early in 1791 he was appointed lieutenant-governor of Upper Canada,* but he did not depart for these new duties until September 1791. His anti-slavery views remained strong, and he stated them forcefully: "The moment that I assume the government of Upper Canada under no modification will I assent to a law that discriminates, by dishonest policy, between the natives of Africa, America, and Asia."[19]

In Canada, Simcoe supported local parliamentary government, the Anglican clergy, better relations with Native Americans, immigration, defense of frontiers, creation of a university and a library, agriculture, and many other initiatives in this developing colony. Many of his plans were fulfilled, but he was unable to begin the university or the library. He encouraged blacks to come to Canada to settle in integrated, not segregated, communities. Though he spoke as an administrator with some humanitarian views, he was welcoming slaves into a society where most of the citizens held racist views, a situation which was eventually bound to lead to strife.[20]

Simcoe was not deterred. In 1793 he learned of the case of Chloe Cooley, a black girl owned by William Vrooman. She had been bound and "violently and forcibly" transported across the border into the United States where she was to be sold. Though slavery was legal in Canada, Simcoe took action. Vrooman was charged with disturbing the

John Graves Simcoe, lieutenant-governor of Upper Canada, supported black refugees (Archives of Ontario).

*Upper Canada became Canada West in 1841 and was renamed Ontario in 1867.

1. Blacks in Canada

peace, even though it could not be sustained by law. Simcoe wanted to influence the public to oppose slavery. He then had a bill calling for the gradual abolition of slavery introduced into the House of Assembly, with its 16 members, six of whom were slave owners. A watered down bill passed, preventing the importation of slaves into Upper Canada. Simcoe was greatly disappointed in the legislation, but word of his support of human rights reached whites and blacks in the United States, and a few blacks from the United States began to flee to Canada, even though they may not have known that slavery was still legal there.

Other high officials in Canada were involved in opposing slavery. William Osgoode, Chief Justice of Lower Canada, ruled in 1803 that slavery was not authorized by British law. Although his ruling did not mean that slavery was officially ended, the 300 or so slaves in his region of Lower Canada were freed. After the War of 1812, blacks were also encouraged to settle in Canada by Sir Peregrine Maitland, lieutenant-governor of Upper Canada, over the objections of U.S. Secretary of State Henry Clay. The word spread in the United States that the Canadian government looked with favor on blacks and that once they reached Canadian soil they were free. What the escapees didn't realize until after they arrived in Canada was that slavery was not officially abolished until 1833 and that racism still persisted in the general population.[21]

There was, however, growing support among Canadian government officials for the rights of all peoples, black and white. "Since freedom of the person [is] the most important civil right protected by the law of England," wrote Upper Canada's Attorney General in 1819, "... the negroes [are] entitled to personal freedom through residence in [Canada] and any attempt to infringe their rights [will] be resisted in the courts."[22]

There were a few exceptions to this statement, and a small number of escaped slaves were actually extradited and returned to slavery in the United States. The courts, however, almost always sided with the slaves, though at times some few fugitives were detained in Canadian jails for a few days before being freed.[23]

The 1837 case of Solomon Moseby (or Mosely) shows how strongly blacks and white government officials felt about attempts to re-enslave fugitives. Solomon had run away from Kentucky, but his master had located him and charged him with stealing a horse. Solomon was jailed at Niagara-on-the Lake; a large number of blacks took him from the jail, and two were killed in the attack. Though he was able to escape, many of those who rescued Solomon were arrested. The courts set them free on the condition that they join the militia. The authorities did not hunt Solomon down and re-arrest him, and they imposed only minor punishment for those who participated in the killing of the two men.

In that same year Jesse Happy, also a slave from Kentucky who was living in Canada, was arrested. Four years earlier, Jesse had taken his master's horse and departed northward. Identified after all those years, Jesse was charged with horse theft, his former master feeling that these were grounds for Happy's unhappy return to Kentucky. Jesse insisted that he rode the horse only a short distance and then sent a message to his master telling him where the horse was. Jesse then followed the North Star, on foot, to Canada. Recognized years later, Happy was jailed and his master began extradition proceedings. Lieutenant-Governor Sir Francis Bond Head decided to refer the matter to Queen Victoria's government. Before a reply was received from London, Sir Francis's Executive Council of Upper Canada decided that there was not sufficient evidence to extradite Happy, and he was freed. Shortly thereafter the British Secretary of State in London came to the same conclusion. Runaway slaves had reason to believe that they were protected by the British lion's paw.[24]

How were refugee slaves and free blacks to live once they arrived in Canada? Some established successful farms, like the Shadds did. A considerable number arrived in abject poverty, literally without possessions. They needed some initial help with housing and housekeeping supplies, warm clothing, and tools to help them make a living — such as axes, hoes, washtubs and irons. They also needed information about where jobs were to be found. Some needed medical attentions. But the refugees wanted to be self-sufficient and most were greatly opposed to begging. Several individuals and societies such as religious organizations set up social service structures to help them. Hiram Wilson (1803–1864), assisted slaves for three decades, and many Underground Railroad conductors sent their passengers to him. He

1. Blacks in Canada

understood the slaves' need for education, and he established schools and recruited teachers. Unfortunately, he was poorly organized and failed in his efforts with Josiah Henson to develop the Dawn Colony for blacks.[25] Isaac Rice, a Presbyterian minister before moving from Ohio to Canada, worked for years with refugees. He too was undisciplined, needing more money than he had and spending more than was in his treasury. He was much gossiped about because he had left his wife, and doctrinal disagreements with other ministers, which obviously limited his effectiveness. He, Henson, and Wilson had to rely on "begging," and soon there were charges that funds were being misused.[26]

The most successful of the charitable organizations for blacks in Canada were local ones which did not depend on "begging" funds from the United States and abroad. One of the best known was True Band, organized first in Malden, Canada West, in 1854 with 600 members. The Chatham, Canada West, society had 375 members enrolled, and in 1855 there were 14 chapters in various parts of Canada West. Black men and women could join the organization, each making a small monthly payment to be used for those in financial need. Blacks in Canada were proud, and they wanted to show "that the colored population possess the means and the will, when acting in concert, to take care of themselves and of the strangers as they arrive." The True Band members were also interested in keeping down strife between the religious groups. They encouraged parents to send their children to school, and attempted "to prevent litigation by referring all disputes among themselves to a committee."[27]

Mrs. Dr. Willis, wife of the professor of theology and principal of Knox College in Toronto was a member of the Toronto Ladies' Association for the Relief of Destitute Colored Fugitives. Women like Mrs. Willis in their societies were involved in making warm clothes for the newly-arriving blacks, and they also helped find housing, made small financial contributions to help the fugitives get started earning a living, and gave advice about where to look for jobs—they might suggest that a friend was in need of a cook, or a gardener, or a woodchopper to lay in a supply of wood for the winter months.[28] Black women also worked cooperatively with this Ladies' Association. Mrs. Willis also worked closely with the Anti-Slavery Society of Canada.

Once Hiram Wilson left Dawn and moved to St. Catharines, he worked through a local organization, the "Refugee Slaves' Friend Society." Small charitable organizations helped refugees most when they were local, providing medical assistance to those who were ill, information about jobs, help with housing, which allowed the blacks to become self-sufficient quickly.

For refugee slaves and free blacks with special skills, such as carpentry, barbering, and blacksmithing, there was certainly work in small towns and cities. Maids, cooks, laundresses, waiters, sailors, and dressmakers could find positions. A few blacks opened businesses, kept hotels, and owned livery services. Some trained to become teachers and physicians. Many of the blacks reaching Canada, though, had worked on plantation fields and because of the climate in their new country they could not use their knowledge of growing cotton, rice, and sugarcane. Some early black settlers found that tobacco was a viable cash crop in parts of Canada West, and blacks from tobacco-growing states in the United States had success with that crop.

Slaves had deliberately been kept in ignorance of book knowledge, but they had learned how to survive. Often badly fed by their masters, they fished and (often secretly) hunted. They grew gardens and raised chickens and pigs. In Canada, they could grow their own food, supplemented with hunting and fishing, and grow cash crops such as wheat, potatoes, vegetables, and fruits for local markets. The railroads were being pushed through, and black men could get jobs with those companies, allowing them to save some money to buy clothes for their families or to make down payments on land.

Government land was available at a low price, but many blacks found it difficult to understand how to complete the paperwork and turned to land speculators who often sold the ex-slaves' property without a proper title. Confidence men drew up contracts which caused the new owners to lose their farms in a few years—after they had cleared the land and made improvements that enhanced the value of the property.

To protect refugees from unscrupulous confidence men and to make it easier for blacks to live in a new country, various groups began thinking of colony schemes. They would raise money to buy a large plot of land; sell small farms to settlers, allowing payments over a number of years; establish schools. These were not utopian or socialist communities—properties were not held in common.

To raise money for most of these colonies, agents were sent to the United States and Britain, but much of the funds raised were used by the agents for their expenses. Some of the funds that arrived in Canada were misused. Most of the colonies were undercapitalized and mismanaged.[29] These were the major colonies:

Wilberforce

Blacks in Cincinnati, distressed by Ohio's Black Code, which made it difficult for them to stay in the state, decided to move to land they were buying near the Canadian town of Lucan. In 1829 and 1830 about 20 families arrived. The colony was always underfunded, and one unscrupulous agent seems to have sold some land for which there was not a clear title. The begging agent misused the funds they raised, and neighbors were prejudiced against blacks and wanted no more settlers, and by 1835 the colony was essentially moribund.[30]

Dawn

Josiah Henson, an AME minister and leader of blacks in Canada West, was joined by Hiram Wilson in founding Dawn, a community on a large plot of land broken into parcels for farms to be paid for over a period of years, a manual training school as well as an elementary school, a sawmill to make use of the heavily-timbered lands the colony owned, and a grist mill. Dawn began in 1842; again the colony depended on raising funds in the United States and abroad. At first the sawmill was successful, but it was allowed to fall into ruin. The manual arts school began but lacked financial support. Quarrels broke out between Henson and other leaders. Much money was poured into Dawn, but it was a terrible failure.[31]

The Refugee Home Society

Isaac Rice and the black minister T. Willis had the idea for the Refugee Home Society in 1846, and five years later Henry Bibb, the black publisher of *Voice of the Fugitive*, and others began serious planning for a land colony which would have schools and churches. Agents were sent out to raise money. Internal and external strife was soon present. Mary Ann Shadd in her newspaper *The Provincial Freeman* led the opposition, charging that Bibb misused the Society funds. Internally, settlers were dissatisfied because the Society land was more expensive than government land and because the Society changed the terms of the land agreement to the disadvantage of the settlers. The Refugee Home Society was another failure, though it survived until the end of the Civil War.[32]

The Elgin Settlement

The most successful of the colonies was founded by the Rev. William King, a well-educated white Presbyterian minister with private funds. He bought land near Chatham, Canada West, for the Elgin Association. He maintained strong control over the colony and the settlers. The settlement had an excellent school system, in which the Rev. King emphasized a classical education as opposed to the Manual Training at Dawn. Although personally an authoritarian, the Rev. King seems to have realized that religious tolerance was called for, and the two most popular churches in the black community — AME and Baptist — were established. Out of the colonies his alone had a post office, allowing settlers more contact with the outside world. The Rev. King recognized the power of block voting and encouraged the settlers to take part in the electoral process. Settlers might chafe at some of the restrictions at Elgin, but their attitudes toward it were mostly positive, and the colony and the settlers there were successful.[33]

Jason H. Silverman's *Unwelcome Guests: Canada West's Response to American Fugitive Slaves, 1800–1865* is a careful and useful study, but the first part of the title is not quite accurate, for the labor and serv-

1. Blacks in Canada

ices of the fugitives were needed in the developing country. Many, undoubtedly most, of the citizens of Canada had deeply-held prejudices against blacks, and also against the Irish, who were poverty stricken and competed for jobs blacks often held. French-speaking Canadians were also prejudiced against blacks but were often not as overt in their actions as the English-speakers were.

Silverman and other scholars have shown how pervasive the prejudices against blacks were. Henry Bibb, the black newspaper editor, exaggerated only slightly when he wrote: "Canadian Negro hate is incomparably MEANER than the Yankee article, for Canadian Negro hat is not ORIGINAL. Copied, aped, deviltry is always meaner than the original diabolism.... A meaner set of negro haters, God in his inexplicable mercy, does not suffer to live, than these poor fools of Canadian second-generation imitations."[34]

Blacks in Canada who were interviewed in the 1850s and early 1860s often spoke of the racism they faced. But Canada was a rapidly developing country then, with farmers, black and white, clearing timber and planting crops, requiring great physical effort. The railroads were being built, and there was a labor shortage only partially filled by the immigrant Irish. Cooks, maids, woodchoppers, painters, carpenters, hostlers, fishermen, freshwater sailors, teachers, and barbers were needed in small towns and in cities. Blacks were opening shops, being successful in business, becoming teachers and newspaper editors, and establishing good farms. Prejudice against blacks was real and pervasive, but black labor and black farmers were needed, and therefore were tolerated.

Freshwater sailors were in demand, and Captain Averill of Malden said of black sailors, "They are the best men we have. We have to pay them the same as white men, and I prefer them to some portion of our citizens [probably a reference to the Irish]. We have to keep them separate from white sailors. We cannot mix them. We always either carry a black crew or a white one." Although the captain praised black sailors, his prejudices were evident. Crews had to be black or white. He complained that blacks spent their money freely and didn't put any aside. The general view was that these sailors worked hard in the summer but "loafed" during the winter. The captain also felt that black sailors had a lower place in the Great Chain of Being: "We never make them mates." The captain probably felt he was an unprejudiced man; after all, he declared, "We can put more confidence in them than we can in white men."[35]

Not to be forgotten, though, is the anti-slavery view of government officials who welcomed refugees from slavery, announced they were free as soon as they were on Canadian soil, and protected them from United States slave catchers. George Brown, editor of the Toronto *Globe*, supported black causes, as did many white clergymen, schoolmasters, and women in the white community. Blacks could become Canadian citizens, own property, and vote. While township schools were often segregated, universities and colleges were open to blacks, who enrolled in teacher training institutions and medical schools.

The exact number of refugee blacks living in Canada in 1861 at the beginning of the Civil War is not known, although figures of 40,000 to 75,000 have been suggested. The census figures in Canada are not accurate, but a number just over 40,000 seems reasonable.[36] There are also no reliable figures on how many blacks left Canada for the United States within five years after the end of the war, but the exodus was large; probably up to two-thirds of that population departed, hoping that their lives would be better now that slavery had been abolished.[37] Unfortunately, these hopes were largely blasted by the end of the nineteenth century.

2

Shadrach

Sherwood Minkins was born a slave in Norfolk, Virginia, date unknown, but probably between the years 1814 and 1822. A religious man, early in his life he took the name Shadrach from the Biblical figure in the Book of Daniel, chapter 3. King Nebuchadnezzar of Babylon discovered that Shadrach, Meshach, and Abednego, three Jewish men who presided over the affairs of his province of Babylon, did not worship his God. The king ordered them to do so, and they refused, saying their God would deliver them. The three were then cast into the fiery furnace, but they survived the flames. The king then spoke: "Blessed be the God of Shadrach, Meshack, and Abednego, who hath sent his angel and delivered his servants that trusted in him..." (verse 28).

In assuming his new name, Shedrach[1] recognized slavery as a fiery furnace and hoped for deliverance. His owners should have suspected that he would not wait for an angel from God to deliver him but would arrange for his own deliverance by running away.

Before he left Norfolk, Shadrach worked in a tavern, a store, and as a servant in a private home.[2] In the spring of 1850 he escaped by ship, probably bribing a sea captain or crew member, and reached Boston by May.[3] He soon got a job working as a waiter at the Cornhill Coffee House located in plain sight in the center of the city.[4] Shadrach was a fugitive at a time when the whole country was agitated by the proposed Compromise of 1850 which had provisions calling for the return of escaped slaves to their owners, even if they were captured in free states.

The Fugitive Slave Act, part of the compromise, was signed into law on September 18, 1850, and in Boston and other cities there was a call to defy the law. Frederick Douglass recommended that the way to trample the Act would be to produce "a half dozen or more dead kidnappers."[5] Southern spies and slave catchers were at work in many free states where fugitive slaves were living. Shadrach was seen, recognized, and reported to his owner. On February 12, 1851, John Caphart, a slave catcher from Norfolk, arrived in Boston with legal papers from Shadrach's owner seeking the arrest of the runaway and his return to slavery. Caphart quietly secured a warrant for Shadrach's arrest, and on February 15 two federal marshals arrested Shadrach at the coffee shop. He was frightened, did not resist, and was rushed to the courthouse. He was once again in a fiery furnace. Word soon spread in the abolitionist and black communities of Boston.[6] Lawyers came to defend the captured man who was described as being about 25, of "bacon color," "stout," and "square built."[7]

George T. Curtis, the commissioner hearing the case, was a strong supporter of the Compromise of 1850 and the Fugitive Slave Act, but he agreed to a postponement of three days. Shadrach's prospects were bleak, for the papers submitted were properly executed. Curtis ordered the courtroom cleared, leaving Shadrach inside with marshals, guards, and the six attorneys planning his defense. The door to the courtroom was closed and secured, but angry blacks were milling around in the hall. Then, Lewis Hayden, a black escapee from Kentucky who had become a clothing merchant in Boston, led the charge on the door. A crowd of blacks gained entry, took over the courtroom, making much noise to add to the disorder. Shadrach, scared and confused, was seized "by the collar and feet" and carried into the street where more blacks had gathered and were cheering and shouting. Black "angels" delivered him from captivity.

The all-black rescuers and their supporters ran with Shadrach from the square, followed by the guards, who stopped their pursuit after a few blocks. Lewis Hayden had Shadrach taken to a safe attic where he remained until late night February 15. Hayden then took him by carriage to Concord, Massachusetts, arriving at 3 A.M., February 16, at the home of the Edwin Bigelows, a local abolitionist couple. Shadrach was sent by train to Montreal, Canada.[8] This was not the usual destination for fugitive slaves, most of whom in the 1850s settled in Canada

2. Shadrach

West in towns and farms just east of Detroit, around the Canadian side of Niagara Falls, or in Toronto. When Shadrach arrived there, only a few dozen blacks lived in Montreal, a cosmopolitan city of French and English speakers. The climate was harsh and wages were low.

The Book of Daniel has little to say about the biblical Shadrach's life after he survived the fiery furnace, noting only that the king "promoted Shadrach, Meshach, and Abednego, in the province of Babylon." We know nothing of Shadrach's personal or professional life in Babylon. Fortunately, we know much more about the escaped slave Shadrach. He told a visitor to Canada in the late summer of 1851 that his first months there were extremely difficult, for he knew no one. For almost two months, he was ill. It is certainly likely that this frightened young man suffered a psychological collapse following his arrest, rescue, and relocation in an almost totally different environment. He probably had some support from his Boston liberators. He began work as a waiter and soon was able to open, with a partner, a modest restaurant. That venture failed when the partner fled, taking the proceeds of the business with him.

Shadrach told an interviewer in September of 1851 that he was happy to be outside the clutches of manhunters and that he would not return to the United States as long as slavery was legal. In fact, he never returned to the country of his birth.

Shadrach, unable to read and write, was a hard-working man. The best thing his rescuers could have done for him after he reached Montreal would have been to provide him with night school tuition. His efforts to establish himself in a new country would have been much easier had he been literate. His lack of an education hampered him, and another restaurant he opened also failed. He was not successful either as a trader.

Shadrach married Mary, a young Irish woman, and they had three children. His son William, about three or four years old, died of "croop" in 1857, and his daughter Eda, two years older than William, died of tuberculosis in 1858. Respiratory diseases and tuberculosis were common illnesses among black children and adults. Many who escaped slavery had been poorly fed for years and had been living in unsanitary conditions. In Canada, fugitives often continued to be poorly fed and housed. Freedom didn't protect them from croup, pneumonia, and tuberculosis. Shadrach and Mary had one other son, who lived on until the 1930s, but he died without issue.

The Minkins family did not live in a black ghetto but in a mixed neighborhood. Eventually Shadrach turned to barbering and appears to have been successful at that pursuit. He was part of a small, hard-working group of semi-skilled workers, including barbers, whitewashers, carpenters, porters, waiters, cooks, and servants, who found steady employment in Canada.

Shadrach took part in black civic events. He was a Canadian who wanted slavery exterminated in the United States, but when the Civil War was over, he did not join the throngs leaving their adopted country. By 1870 only a few blacks remained in Montreal. Shadrach died in 1875 and is buried in an unmarked grave in the Protestant Cemetery on Mount Royal.[9]

No photograph of Shadrach has survived. The few interviews with him are brief. Unlike many black expatriates in Canada, he put down deep roots and gave his allegiance to the British crown. He was a productive, working-class man who came to Canada frightened and ill and later had a good life in his new country, something not possible for him in the United States.

3

Josiah Henson and Eliza Harris

> A missionary among the fugitives in Canada told us that many of the fugitives confessed themselves to have escaped from comparatively kind masters, and that they were induced to brave the perils of escape, in almost every case, by the desperate horror with which they regarded being sold south, — a doom which was hanging either over themselves or their husbands, their wives or children. This nerves the African, naturally patient, timid, and unenterprising, with heroic courage, and leads him to suffer hunger, cold, pain, the perils of the wilderness, and the more dread penalties of recapture.[1]
> — Harriet Beacher Stowe, *Uncle Tom's Cabin*

Shadrach's escape from slavery, his capture, rescue, and flight to Canada were praised and deplored throughout the North and South during the early years of excitement after the passage of the Fugitive Slave Act of 1850. Shadrach's story was soon eclipsed by Harriet Beecher Stowe's novel *Uncle Tom's Cabin*, serialized in 1851 and published in book form in 1852. It was the first abolitionist fiction to gain a wide readership. Stowe's account of the horrors and brutalities of slavery "left readers by the millions seething with anger and shame,"[2] Fergus M. Bordewich has argued in *Bound for Canaan*. Her novel had phenomenal sales in the United States and abroad, where it appeared in 22 languages. Sometimes realistic, often sentimental, the novel, though filled with Christian piety, also contains vivid scenes of cruelty to slaves and flights for freedom. The novel brought abolition from the margins of national life in the United States into the mainstream, one more push toward war in the volatile 1850s.[3]

The novel has two main plotlines. One is devoted to the pious slave Uncle Tom who refuses to run away even though he knows he is to be sold away down South. He also refuses to murder his master, Simon Legree, in order to gain freedom. Stowe features Uncle Tom in a series of events showing him to be a near-perfect Christian who finally dies at the hands of the villainous Simon Legree. Uncle Tom is a composite character, and Stowe seems to have used some details from the life of the black minister Josiah Henson in her fictional Uncle Tom. Henson, like the fictional Uncle Tom, was a religious man who as a young man refused to run away when he could and, in fact, kept 18 others from gaining freedom. Ironically, Stowe ignores many stories about Henson's later life. He eventually did run away, and he and his family made it to Canada. There he was active in working for his people, but he also mismanaged funds raised for the Dawn colony he had helped establish. In his later years he claimed to be the one and only Uncle Tom of the novel, but this claim is an overstatement.

The second major plotline concerns the slave Eliza who escapes from Kentucky with her young son by crossing the Ohio River on the ice floes, a story based on a daring escape recounted to Stowe by the Ohio abolitionist John Rankin. After a series of adventures on the Underground Railroad, the fictional Eliza reaches Canada, then Paris, and is last seen on the way to Africa where her husband will be a teacher of Christianity.[4] The real Eliza did escape on the ice floes, reached Canada with her son, and returned later to rescue her daughter and her grandchildren.

Following are the stories of Josiah Henson and Eliza Harris. Both followed the North Star to Canada. Henson failed to develop the Dawn colony for his fellow fugitive slaves in Canada West, but he was lionized abroad and was even brought to meet Queen Victoria. Eliza lived in obscurity, and we know little of her life in Canada. She is, however, a sympathetic character in fiction and real life.

Josiah Henson[5]

Josiah Henson (1789–1883), was born a slave in Charles County, Maryland, and he began to see the cruel side of slavery during his childhood. The overseer on the plantation where his mother was hired

3. Josiah Henson and Eliza Harris

Reverend Josiah Henson, one of the founders of the Dawn colony which showed great promise but eventually failed, successfully represented the black cause. Harriet Beecher Stowe in *Uncle Tom's Cabin* used stories about Henson's life in the character Uncle Tom (Uncle Tom's Cabin Museum).

out "brutally assaulted" her. Josiah's father came to her assistance and during the fight struck the white overseer. As punishment, Henson's father was given a hundred lashes, his right ear was nailed to the whipping-post and then severed. Josiah was later to recall that his father had previously been "good humored" and "light hearted," a banjo player who took part in the frolics in the black quarter, but after that brutal punishment he changed and became "Sullen, morose, and dogged, nothing could be done with him."[6] He was sold down South to Alabama, and Josiah and his mother never heard from him again. Josiah saw the effects of fighting the slavery system, and some of his early unwillingness to rebel can undoubtedly be traced to this incident.

Josiah's mother and her children were returned to the plantation of her owner, Dr. McPherson, a benevolent man but a heavy drinker who, in a drunken stupor, drowned in a stream of water not a foot deep. Henson's mother and his siblings were then auctioned off, she going to a man named Isaac Riley, a blacksmith. She begged Riley to purchase Josiah, her baby, to let her keep at least one of her children. Riley refused, struck and kicked her, and Josiah was sold to a man named Robb, a tavern-keeper who owned a stageline and horses. Josiah was taken to Robb's slave quarters where his brutalized slaves took no notice of the child even when he was extremely ill. Afraid the child would not live, Robb sold him to Riley for a small sum, to be worked out by horse shoeing. Reunited with his mother, Josiah recovered and grew into a strong, athletic young man who served Riley, a "course and vulgar" man,[7] for many years, eventually becoming an overseer on the plantation. Henson was always looking for the main chance. He worked hard, seeking approval from his owner, and he served Riley's interests, not those of his fellow slaves. He took on managerial duties and received better and more food. He was a pious slave, having been converted to Christianity when he was about 18. At this stage of his life, he followed one dictate of his religion: servant, obey your master, accept the miseries of this world and expect a better life in the hereafter.

In his autobiography Henson does not adequately address the ethical issue of a black man acting as an overseer of slaves. His fight for a better life allowed him to ignore the needs of his fellow blacks while he kept up the pretense of working for their benefit. His actions were approved by his white owner, and he was rewarded by being allowed to take goods to market and to handle money. Riley, however, often cursed his black overseer.

When Henson was 19 or 20, one of his jobs was to accompany his dissipated master to the cock fights and horse races on weekends, days which were filled with drinking and often ended in brawls. Henson and other attendant slaves were to rush into the melee and get their masters out of danger and on the way home. At one of the donnybrooks, Riley quarreled with Bryce Litton, his brother's overseer. Henson joined the scuffle, and in the fight the drunken Litton was injured and blamed Henson. A week later, on an isolated stretch of road, Litton and three blacks surrounded Josiah. Josiah fought the blacks, but Litton came at him with a stick, battering his head, knocking him down, calling, "Won't you give up! Won't you give up!" and striking his arm and breaking it. Henson fell to the ground headfirst, and Litton lashed out at the slave's back, breaking both shoulder blades. Finally, Litton told the beaten man "to learn what it was to strike a white man."[8]

Henson was in great pain, but Riley did not send for a physician, for he believed "A nigger will get well anyway." Riley's sister bound up Henson's wounds and broken bones, but his arm and shoulder blades did not heal properly. He was never again able to raise his arms over his head. Henson in his autobiography writes that he went through the rest of his life "maimed and mutilated."[9]

3. Josiah Henson and Eliza Harris

With the aid of ghost writers (he himself could barely read and write), Henson continued revising and enlarging his autobiography, which was originally published in 1849. He was a raconteur with a faulty memory as he grew older, but in the account of his early life he seems to have captured the essence of the events he was reporting.

Modern readers, however, may have difficulty understanding Josiah's passivity and meekness during his young adulthood when he was badly treated by white men. Immediately after detailing the terrible beating by Litton and the indifference of Riley to his suffering, Henson wrote that the retained his situation as overseer, "together with the especial favor of my master."[10] Given Riley's refusal to call a physician to set Josiah's broken bones, one wonders how Henson would have been treated if he had been out of Riley's favor.

Henson does admit that he may have cheated Riley by providing better food to his fellow slaves, but he insists that he was always honest in handling Riley's money: "For many years I was his factotum.... I had no reason to think highly of his moral character; but it was my duty to be faithful to him in the position in which he placed me; and I can boldly declare, before God and man, that I was so. I forgave him the causeless blows and injuries he had inflicted on me in my childhood and youth, and was proud of the favor he now showed me, and of the character and reputation I had earned by strenuous and persevering efforts."[11] It is unfortunate that we do not have the testimony of the slaves on the Riley farm about Josiah's activities as overseer of slave-driver. Black overseers were often as hated as the white ones.

Henson, illiterate at this time, was intelligent and enterprising, and more than one modern reader may well think that instead of accepting his bad treatment he should have struck out for Philadelphia. But Josiah did not flee. He stayed and married at the age of 22. About this time, Riley, at 45, married a young woman of 18, and had some legal trouble with his brother-in-law. Entangled in the court system, Riley drank more heavily and became morose and erratic in his behavior.

One night, after Henson had gone to bed in his cabin, Riley arrived in a pitiful state, moaning and wringing his hands.

"Sick, massa?"

The moaning continued.

"Can't I help you in any way, massa?"

"Oh Sie [Henson's nickname, sometimes spelled Si]; I'm ruined, ruined!"

"How so, massa?"

"They've got judgment against me, and in less than two weeks every nigger I've got will be put up and sold."

After cursing his brother-in-law and lamenting his diminishing fortunes, Riley added, "And now, Sie, there is only one way I can save anything. You can do it; won't you, won't you."

Riley wanted Henson to agree to the plan before knowing what it was, and Josiah agreed.

"I want you to run away, Sie, to your master Amos in Kentucky, and take all the servants with you."[12]

Henson undertook this illegal and unethical assignment, calling into question his religious beliefs. In February of 1825 he guided 18 blacks plus his wife and their two children over a route completely unknown to him. As usual, he was resourceful in carrying out his role as overseer. Once the blacks were on the Ohio River with the free state of Ohio on their right, his piety, his religious belief in serving the Lord by serving the wishes of a slave master completely overrode any concern he might have felt for the slaves in his care. Blacks in Ohio on the shore were calling out to the unshackled slaves in the coffle going down the river advising them to remain in a free state instead of going on to Kentucky: "They told us we were fools to think of going on and surrendering ourselves to a new owner; that now we could be our own masters, and put ourselves out of all reach of pursuit."[13] Henson refused to listen to the free blacks and convinced his charges to go on to Kentucky. Henson wrote that he always wanted to be free, but he thought he would purchase himself, his wife, and children. On the slaves went, arriving at Amos's plantation the middle of April 1825.

At the plantation owned by Amos Riley, Henson was again overseer, though he refers in his autobiography to himself as "superintendent." During the next three years, he heard white and black preachers, and in 1828 he became a preacher in the African Methodist Episcopal (AME) Church. That same year Isaac Riley, his owner in

3. Josiah Henson and Eliza Harris

Maryland, decided that the slaves Henson had guided to Kentucky should be sold down South. Only Henson, his wife, and children were to be spared.[14] Henson was to return to Maryland with the proceeds of the sale. Again, what Henson agreed to do was illegal, for there was a court order involving this human "property" illegally moved to Kentucky. Henson's principles continued to be elastic.

At the same time, by way of justifying his involvement in the sale of 18 slaves who had trusted him and were now being sold down the river, Henson wrote in his autobiography, "From that hour I saw through, hated, and cursed the whole system of slavery,"[15] and he vowed to free himself, his wife, and his children. This vow was probably made somewhat later, for Sie went on being the compliant slave. At this period in his life, he fit the classic definition of an Uncle Tom: a term of contempt for a black whose behavior toward whites is servile or fawning.

Harriet Beecher Stowe was particularly impressed with Henson's long-suffering Christian perseverance in slavery, his refusal to resort to violence to defend or free himself. At the beginning of *Uncle Tom's Cabin* there is a scene in which Uncle Tom is told that he is about to be sold because of the financial difficulties of his owner. Instead of running away from Kentucky to Ohio, he decides to stay and be sent away with a slave dealer who will sell him somewhere down south: "Mas'r always found me on the spot, — he always will. I never have broke trust, nor used my pass no ways contrary to my word, and I never will. It's better for me alone to go, than to break up the place and sell all."[16]

Henson, like the fictional Uncle Tom, went on being a dutiful servant. With money in hand from the sale of the slaves, he started out to return to Isaac Riley's home, preaching along the way and receiving church offerings which allowed him to buy a horse and good clothes. Once he arrived back in Maryland, his new possessions irritated Isaac Riley. Henson began to negotiate the purchase of his freedom, and in March of 1829, as Josiah was ready to return to Amos's plantation in Kentucky, the two men agreed that Josiah would buy himself for $450 — $350 in cash and the last $100 as a promissory note.

Once back in Kentucky, Henson learned again just how duplicitous the brothers Riley were. Amos told Henson he owed hundreds of dollars more, not the one hundred agreed upon in Maryland.[17] This story of trickery was common and often mentioned in slave narratives. Sie did not flee.

Soon Amos's son, also named Amos, about 21, was to take a flat-boat filled with goods down the Ohio and Mississippi rivers to New Orleans, and the senior Amos told Sie to go along. Sie suspected that he was probably to be sold once the boat reached New Orleans, even though he had made the initial payment of $350 for his freedom. Like the fictional Uncle Tom, Sie did not run.[18]

The flat-boat stopped at towns and cities along the Ohio and Mississippi rivers to sell goods. At Vicksburg, Sie went to a plantation where many of the slaves he had convinced not to run away to freedom in Ohio were now overworked and underfed. He wrote, "No hell could equal the misery they described as their daily portion. Toiling half naked in malarious marshes, under a burning, maddening sun, and poisoned by swarms of musquitoes and black gnats, they looked forward to death as their only deliverance."[19]

Josiah saw the misery he had helped call down on his fellow slaves, but he did not flee into the thickets along the river. Instead, agitated by his realization at what he had done and what had befallen him, he thought of killing his companions on the boat, taking their money, scuttling the flat-boat, and starting out for the North. Not far from New Orleans, on a rainy night, all were asleep except Sie, and he took an axe and was ready to kill young Amos. He raised the ace "to strike the fatal blow, — when suddenly the thought came to me, 'What! commit *murder!* and you a Christian?'" He had previously thought of his contemplated action as self-defense but was not filled "with shame and remorse," and he resigned himself to God's will and put the axe down.[20]

In *Uncle Tom's Cabin* Stowe reworked that scene with an important change. On Simon Legree's plantation where the master is characterized as evil and vicious, the female slave Cassy, once Simon's concubine (and, we later learn, Eliza Harris's mother), tells Uncle Tom that Simon is in a brandy-induced sleep, and the axe is ready to do him in. She would have done the deed herself, but her arms were weak.

3. Josiah Henson and Eliza Harris

"'Not for ten thousand worlds, Misse!' said Tom, firmly, stopping and holding her back, as she was pressing forward.

"'But think of all these poor creatures,' said Cassy. 'We might set them all free, and go somewhere in the swamps, and find an island, and live by ourselves. I've heard of its being done. Any life is better than this.'"

"'No!' said Tom firmly. 'No! good never comes of wickedness. I'd sooner chop my right hand off!'"

"'Then *I* will do it,' said Cassy, turning."

"'Oh, Misse Cassy!' said Tom, throwing himself before her, 'for the dear Lord's sake that died for ye, don't sell your precious soul to the devil, that way! Nothing but evil will come of it. The Lord hasn't called us to wrath. We must suffer, and wait his time.'"[21]

Stowe did not allow Uncle Tom to have the idea of the axe murder as Henson did, before rejecting it.

Mrs. Stowe was usually vague when she spoke of her use of incidents in Henson's life in *Uncle Tom's Cabin*. She was more specific than usual in a letter of June 18, 1877, published in the *Windsor Daily Record*, when she wrote: "It is also true that a sketch of his life, published many years ago by the Massachusetts Anti-Slavery Society, furnished me many of the finest conceptions and incidents of Uncle Tom's character ... in particular the scene where he refuses to free himself by the murder of a brutal master. The real history of Josiah Henson in some points goes even beyond that of Uncle Tom in traits of heroic manhood. He once visited me in Andover, and personal intercourse confirmed the high esteem I had for him...."[22]

Once the boat was in New Orleans and the goods sold, young Amos set out to sell Sie. Planters came to consider the slave, inspecting him minutely as if he were a farm animal. Amos kept saying he wanted to find a good master for Sie, one who needed a coachman or house servant, but this was mere talk. Amos wanted to make the sale and return home. Sie was to be sold the next day, but Amos became violently ill and begged Henson to stay with him: "Stick to me, Sie! Stick to me, Sie! Don't leave me. I'm sorry I was going to sell you."[23] Sie stayed, nursing Amos on the boat taking them back up the river. Amos, once home, recovered slowly and continued to appreciate what

Sie had done for him. The senior Amos and other members of his family did not see a ministering slave who saved the life of young Amos; instead they saw dollar signs. Sie knew another attempt to sell him would soon be made. After years of mistreatment, Henson finally decided to flee to Canada.[24]

Josiah now had a wife and four children. At first, his wife was reluctant to run away. She had not been treated as badly as he had and did not have, he insisted, the same longing for freedom that he had. There is little evidence that he had given thought to fleeing during the many years of mistreatment, and over the years he must have justified to his wife his acceptance of his lot in life. Her fears were real ones that were felt throughout the slave quarters: "We shall die in the wilderness; we shall be hunted down with bloodhounds; we shall be brought back and whipped to death." Sie said of her fears and apprehensions: "She was a poor, ignorant, unreasoning woman."[25] She may have been poor and ignorant, but she was not unreasoning. She had four young children to protect.

Sie was an authoritarian who believed in the adage "Wife, follow your husband." He demanded the subservience of his wife and children and the slaves he oversaw. The former slave Lewis Clarke was right when he observed that "favorite slaves"—and Henson belonged to this category all the years he acted as overseer—were pitiful creatures: "They are obliged to cringe a little lower than any of the others."[26]

The authoritarian husband finally prevailed, and Henson's wife agreed to run away, but there was the problem of the two youngest children, two and three years old, who would need to be carried. Sie's wife made a knapsack of tow-cloth with shoulder straps, and the two small children were to be carried on his back.[27]

One dark night in the middle of September 1830, the six Hensons made ready to depart. Tom, the oldest son, was staying with the elder Amos Riley, and through a ruse Sie had brought him home with the excuse that his mother needed to mend his clothes. The Hensons reached the Ohio River, and a fellow slave rowed them over to the Indiana shore. They had no friends to help them in this free state; they knew no abolitionists, no Quakers to turn to for help. The Under-

3. Josiah Henson and Eliza Harris

The Henson family escaped from slavery in Kentucky, with Josiah carrying the two small boys on his back (University of Florida Libraries).

ground Railroad was still in its early years of existence and Henson knew no conductors on that line.

Without a road map, the Henson family headed away from Kentucky, sleeping by day hidden in the underbrush, and walking by night, on the way to Canada, following the light at the end of the gou'd. There was danger everywhere, wild animals in the woods, bounty hunters willing to cut short their dash for freedom for a few shekels. They had too little food and the children cried from hunger. Some farmers that Henson approached offering to buy food refused, one saying, "No, I [have] nothing for niggers."[28] In one incident, though, the farmer's wife did give him venison and bread and refused his quarter. The meat was salty, and the children were soon thirsty. Josiah tried to bring them water in his hat, but it had holes in it. His shoes were intact. He washed them out and carried water in them to his family.

33

Finally, somewhat off course, the Hensons reached Cincinnati, where they were taken in by what Henson called Good Samaritans, apparently abolitionists. To protect their identity he does not indicate how he found them or how long they sheltered the runaways. The Underground Railroad was growing, and the Hensons were taken 30 miles north by wagon; they then continued their walking at night and hiding by day.[29] At a later time, the secret rail line would have taken them all the way to Canada.

Somewhere in Ohio, the Hensons came upon a band of Native Americans, as frightened by blacks as the blacks were of the so-called "red men." The Hensons were taken to a stately man who seemed to be the chief, and he assured his braves that they should not be afraid of these dark-skinned people. The Indians took them in for the night, gave them food and a wigwam for shelter. The next day, the friendly Indians told them that Lake Erie was about 25 miles away and showed them the road to take.[30]

The Hensons soon reached the outskirts of Sandusky, Ohio, and Josiah left his family in hiding and walked to the lake, where he saw a schooner being loaded.

"Hollo, there, man! You want to work?" cried out the captain.

"Yes, sir!"

"Come along, come along; I'll give you a shilling an hour. Must get off with this wind. Oh, you can't work; you're crippled." In addition to Henson's badly-healed shoulder blades and arm, he had carried the two small children in a knapsack and had worn the skin off his back.

"Can't I," Henson said, and picked up a bag of corn, taking his place in the line of workers.

"How far is it to Canada?" he asked the black man next to him in line, and the man immediately knew that Josiah was a fugitive slave.

"Want to go to Canada? Come along with us, then. Our captain's a fine fellow. We're going to Buffalo."

"Buffalo; how far is that from Canada?"

"Don't you know, man? Just across the river."

Henson then explained that his family was nearby.

"I'll speak to the captain," his companion said.

The captain took Henson aside: "The Doctor [black cooks were

3. Josiah Henson and Eliza Harris

given the courtesy title of doctor] says you want to go to Buffalo with your family."

"Yes, sir."

"Well, why not go with me! Doctor says you've got a family."

"Yes, sir."

"Where do they stop?"

"About a mile back."

"How long have you been there?"

"No time."

"Come, my good fellow, tell us all about it. You're running away ain't you?" Henson recognized him as a friend and told his story.

"How long will it take you to get ready?"

"Be here in half an hour, sir."

"Well, go along and get them."

Josiah started, only to hear the captain call out, "Stop, you go on getting the grain in. When we get off, I'll lay to over opposite that island, and send a boat back. There's a lot of regular nigger-catchers in the town below, and they might suspect you if you brought your party out of the bush by daylight."

Henson returned and helped finish the loading of two or three hundred bushels of corn, the hatches were fastened, and the ship sailed.[31]

Henson's reactions as the ship left the dock are the most poetic in his autobiography, and we present the passage as free verse:

> I watched the vessel with intense interest as she left her
>   moorings.
> Away she went before the free breeze.
> Already she seemed beyond the spot at which the captain
>   agreed to lay to,
> and still she flew along.
> My heart sank within me,
> so near deliverance,
> and again to have my hoped blasted,
> again to be cast on my own resources!
> I felt that they had been making a mock of my misery.
> The sun had sunk to rest,
> and the purple and gold of the west were fading away into grey.
> Suddenly, however, as I gazed with a weary heart,
> the vessel swung round into the wind,

the sails flapped,
and she stood motionless.

A moment more, and a boat was lowered from her stern,
and with steady stroke made for the point at which I stood.
I felt that my hour of release had come.
On she came,
and in ten minutes she rode up handsomely on the beach.[32]

Two sailors and Doctor, the black man who had befriended Henson, jumped from the small boat, and the four of them went in search of Josiah's family. At first, they could not be found; his wife thought he had been captured and that slave-catchers were bringing her husband back to the hiding area in order to capture her and the children. Henson had referred to his wife as "ignorant and unreasoning," but she seemed to have been quite competent in this incident, hiding herself and her children from what she perceived as danger. Finally the confusion was sorted out, and they all returned to the ship, where they were greeted with three cheers.[33]

The captain, who was Scottish, called out: "Coom up on deck, and clop your wings and craw like a rooster; you're a free nigger as sure as the devil."*[34]

Henson wept with happiness. He was a man of vast ego, and he failed to give the reactions of his wife and older children.

The next evening, the ship reached Buffalo.

"You see those trees," the captain said to Josiah the next morning, "they grow on free soil, and as soon as your feet touch that, you're a *mon*. I want to see you go and be a freeman. I'm poor myself, and have nothing to give you; I only sail the boat for wages; but I'll see you across. Here, Green," he said, to a ferryman, "What will you take this man and his family over for — he's got no money."

"Three shillings."

The captain handed over a dollar, put his hand on Henson's head, and said, "Be a good fellow, won't you?"

Henson responded, "I'll use my freedom well; I'll give my soul to God."[35]

---

*The Scottish captain speaks standard English earlier.

3. Josiah Henson and Eliza Harris

When the Henson family reached Canada West, Henson threw himself on the ground, celebrating freedom (University of Florida Libraries).

The Hensons reached Canadian soil on October 28, 1830. Josiah did more than crow like a rooster: "I threw myself on the ground, rolled in the sand, seized handfuls of it and kissed them, and danced around, till, in the eyes of several who were present, I passed for a madman."

"He's some crazy fellow," a Colonel Warren observed.

"Oh, no, master! don't you know? I'm free." Henson was still clinging to old ways even as he was free; he calls the colonel "master."

Colonel Warren burst out laughing and said, "Well, I never knew freedom make a man roll in the sand in such a fashion."[36] The colonel obviously did not recognize the emotionalism found in many black church services.

Henson kissed his wife and children, and for a time went on with his exuberance.

The Henson family was free.

Henson had always moved easily in the white world, and once he arrived in Canada he immediately began to look about in the white world for opportunities. He approached a Mr. Hibbard, a wealthy farmer, who lived six or seven miles inland from the lake and struck a bargain to work for him. Hibbard allowed the Hensons to move into a two story shanty on the farm. Pigs had broken into the lower floor and had been living there. Henson worked until midnight cleaning the floor and then brought his family to their new home the next day. There was no furniture. Henson begged straw from his employer, used logs in the corners of the room to confine the straw, and there they slept in comfort.[37]

Henson's wife and children soon became seriously ill, caused, he felt, by "the great exposures we had been through." Fleeing fugitives suffered physically and emotionally, and it was common for them to collapse for a time after they arrived in a safe place. The five sick Hensons survived their illnesses.[38]

Henson made himself useful on the farm and soon had the trust of Hibbard; Henson was following his usual pattern of ingratiating himself to a white man who had power over him. Mrs. Henson and Mrs. Hibbard became friends, and the family began to acquire necessary household goods. Mrs. Hibbard undoubtedly passed on cooking utensils and used clothing to Mrs. Henson. Winter was coming and the Hensons needed warm clothes.

Henson undoubtedly worked on salary the first year or two and then on shares. He began to acquire farm animals—pigs, a cow, and a horse. The lives of the Hensons were improving: they could grow their own food and they were sheltered better than they had been in Kentucky, for they now had a plank floor instead of dirt. Henson also returned to preaching, and this added small sums to his income.

Henson preached, but his biblical knowledge was limited. He could not read, but he writes that he had a good memory and listened to many sermons and heard many biblical verses quoted. After the Hensons arrived in Canada, he had a chance to learn to read, but he essentially failed. Hibbard paid for two quarters of tuition for Henson's son Tom, and the schoolmaster taught Tom for some additional quarters without pay.[39] Tom quickly became a good reader, and on Sunday mornings, before Henson was to preach, Tom read biblical passages to him.

Tom would ask, "Where shall I read, father?"

"Anywhere, my son," he would respond, not knowing, according to his autobiography, "how to direct him," showing how little he knew about the Bible.

Tom opened the Bible to Psalm 103 (A Psalm of David), reading: "Bless the Lord, O my soul, and all that is within me, bless his holy name." The 22 verses, noted the headnote in the King James version used by Tom, are "An exhortation to bless God for his mercy." The God of Psalms 103 was "slow to anger and plenteous in mercy." After he heard these lines, Henson thought of "the dangers and afflictions from which the Lord had delivered me, and compared my present condition with what it had been." Henson was overcome with emotion but was soon returned to reality for Tom asked, "Father, who was David? He writes pretty, don't he? Who was David?"

Henson did not know; he had never heard of David. He answered, "He was a man of God, my son."

"I suppose so, but I want to know something more about him. Where did he live? What did he do?"

Henson had to admit to his son that he did not know who David was and that he could not read. He was completely ignorant of the biblical accounts of David.[40]

Henson always insisted that he had a retentive mind and remembered what he had heard in sermons. Is it possible he never heard a sermon quoting from the Psalms? For a preacher, Henson's biblical knowledge was scanty.

Tom offered to teach his father to read, for it would, Tom knew, make him "talk better and preach better."[41] Henson agreed to try, but he was a slow learner. Studying winter nights he learned to read a little, but it seemed he did not read well. Biblical literature, news of the day, political matters of concern to blacks in the United States and Canada came to him from other people. Henson was an intelligent man in many ways, but it is likely that he did not want to change his illiterate state in any meaningful way. In later years, he used his illiteracy effectively when he characterized his life in slavery which had left him in this state; but, his effectiveness as a speaker and his worldly knowledge was handicapped by his inability to read well.

At the end of three years, Henson began to work for a Mr. Riseley, who lived a few miles away from the Hibbard farm. According to Henson, Riseley had superior abilities and a more elevated mind than Hibbard. Henson had become aware that most of the escaped slaves in the neighborhood worked for hire and did not make an effort to take up land of their own to become self-reliant and self-sufficient. Riseley allowed Henson to call a meeting of blacks at the Riseley home to consider establishing colonies of blacks on "wild lands, which we could call our own, and where every tree which we felled and every bushel of corn we raised, would be for ourselves, in other words, where we could secure all the profits of our own labor." In 1834 Henson set out to find the right spot for such a colony.[42]

In the black community where the needs were great, Henson was becoming a leader. Newly-arriving, penniless refugees needed some immediate help with housing, clothing, and advice about jobs. They needed to know about schooling for their children. Those runaways who wanted to farm needed to know that local farmers and land speculators often cheated illiterate blacks by renting them land and then reclaiming it after the trees had been cleared and other improvements had been made.[43] Black farmers, new and old, needed to be warned not to rely on one crop. At one time, tobacco was an important crop for black farmers in Canada, but the market eventually crashed.[44]

Henson was a farm laborer and minister who believed that he could aid his fellow blacks in Canada by being part social worker for the new arrivals and part county agent to help farmers get started, advising them on the best crops for the short growing season. He was a convincing speaker with an important message about the evils of slavery. He was not, however, the right man for the responsibilities he took on in establishing a colony, for he did not read well and could not himself interpret contracts and land deeds. He was inclined to develop grandiose plans and then leave the difficult details to others. He was also involved in too many activities and was poorly organized.[45]

3. Josiah Henson and Eliza Harris

Henson began to search for areas where he and his followers could purchase their own land. In 1834 he settled a small colony on land near Colchester, but he did not discover that the title to their purchase was not clear, and the colonists had to apply to the legislature for relief. In 1836, during the stay at Colchester, Henson met Hiram Wilson, and the two were to work together for several years.

Hiram Wilson was born in 1803 in New Hampshire and studied at the Oneida Institute which emphasized academic subjects and manual labor. He was strongly opposed to slavery, but he learned after he enrolled in the Lane Seminary in Cincinnati to study theology that the trustees did not allow the faculty and students to participate in abolitionist activities. He and several other "radicals" left for the more liberal Oberlin, and he received his degree in theology in 1836. A gift of $25 allowed him to travel to Canada to study the conditions of escaped slaves there, and he began decades of work in Canada West. He established more than a dozen schools, recruiting teachers for them. He was a formidable money raiser among American philanthropists, but unfortunately he was a poor organizer and manager.[46]

Henson and Wilson began to make plans for a colony named Dawn, specifically for blacks, near Chatham, Canada West. They raised money and bought land in 1841. The plan called for establishing a manual training school to be named "The British American Institute." Elementary education was also to be offered.

Settlers arrived, and the school at Dawn opened in 1842. At first, the colony seemed successful. The Institute grew for a time, and Wilson and Henson developed forward-looking educational plans. The Dawn property had excellent timber on it, and funds were raised to build a sawmill, but after initial successes the colony began to have major problems. The school floundered. The sawmill was allowed to fall into disuse. There were legal disputes and charges of financial malfeasance. Henson was charged several times with misusing funds, and although he was always cleared, his local reputation was damaged. He was genuinely concerned about the conditions of black refugees in Canada, but he tended to be prodigal with funds brought in by "begging." Poorly organized, he did not keep careful account of Dawn funds.

Wilson, also, was not an efficient manager. A founder of schools and a self-appointed social worker trying to meet the needs of penniless refugees, he always needed money. He begged for money and consistently spent more than was in his treasury.

Dawn had two ineffective managers, and as the internal disputes escalated, Wilson withdrew and moved to St. Catharines where he continued to aid refugees.[47]

As Dawn floundered, Henson became as passive as he had been in slavery and did little to save the colony. At the same time, paradoxically, Henson became well-known and admired throughout Canada, the United States, and England. He had dictated his autobiography to Samuel A. Eliot in 1849. Later, John Lobb of England took over as Henson's ghostwriter and introduced many exaggerations and questionable stories into an edition which then had large sales.[48]

Harriet Beecher Stowe read Henson's story some time before she wrote *Uncle Tom's Cabin*, and used parts of it selectively in creating the character Uncle Tom. The novel was published to great acclaim in book form in 1852, but many readers questioned the accuracy of her presentation of slaves and slavery. She then published in 1853 *A Key to Uncle Tom's Cabin* and mentioned Henson's slave narrative as one of her sources. After the stories began to circulate that Josiah Henson was Uncle Tom, Mrs. Stowe was asked several times for verification, and she continued to acknowledge her use of Henson's story.[49] It is clear, however, that she relied on several sources in the writing of the life of the fictional Uncle Tom.

Early on, Henson seems to have avoided claiming too much about his part in the novel. Certainly readers of his narrative could see that Stowe chose to take from his life story his Christian piety, his unwillingness for many years to flee from slavery, his keeping other slaves from vanishing into the free state of Ohio, and his refusal to kill young Amos on the trip to New Orleans. In Stowe's novel, Uncle Tom was sold down the river and died a terrible death at the hands of Simon Legree. In Henson's slave narrative, he and his family escaped to Canada. Henson's last ghost writer, however, began to claim that Uncle Tom and Henson were the same person, a tactic certain to sell copies of the autobiography, and Henson seems to have come to believe this half-truth.

3. Josiah Henson and Eliza Harris

Henson traveled to England three times, was feted by the aristocracy, and presented to Queen Victoria. He was now the real, the only, Uncle Tom. Dawn, though, withered away, all the "begged" money used to sustain it did too little to help black refugees. Blacks would undoubtedly have been better off to have rejected colony life, which was poorly-run and segregated, and to have bought government land on their own. In spite of prejudice against them, they could have lived, in many instances, in an integrated society, for their services and their food crops were needed.

Henson's life and actions in two of the three main periods of his life are questionable: In his early life he was obsequious, a tool of his owner, an overseer who kept fellow slaves from gaining freedom. In the middle period of his life he showed great skill in freeing his family and getting them established in Canada. In his third phase, however, when he became a colony founder, he did not have the education or skills to be successful. Though Dawn was a failure, he was a powerful speaker who pointed out the evils of slavery, and he was rightly honored for that work. He was skilled in raising money, but the funds were often misspent.

William L. Andrews in *To Tell a Free Story* argues that Henson's "reconstruction of his life in slavery was a kind of morality play in which the best and worst sides of him were pitted against each other for control of his character and destiny."[50] Henson had best and worst sides, but Mrs. Stowe created the character of Uncle Tom with only one side — the best.

Eliza Harris

The most famous fictional black who escaped slavery and made it to Canada was Eliza Harris in Harriet Beecher Stowe's *Uncle Tom's Cabin*. On a trip to Kentucky, Stowe attended church. She wrote, "While there, her attention was called to a beautiful quadroon girl, who sat in one of the slips of the church and appeared to have charge of some young children. The description of Eliza may suffice for a description of her."[51] This is the description of the young and beautiful Eliza in the first chapter of *Uncle Tom's Cabin*: "silky black hair," "rich, full" eyes, a brown complexion showing a flush when the slave trader gave her admiring, sexual glances, and a "finely moulded shape." From this "portrait drawn from life,"[52] Stowe added the story of the real person, whose name in slavery is unknown, who braved the ice floes to escape with her son. The best account of the actual Eliza is in Ann Hagedorn's *Beyond the River*, and we are much indebted to the careful research in that volume.

On a cold late February night in 1838 a mulatto woman soon to be given the name Eliza, fearing that her owner was going to sell some of his slaves, including her two-year-old son, ran away. She was a mature woman with grandchildren. Taking her son with her, she quietly departed from a farm near Dover, Kentucky. She ran to the nearby Ohio River, which had been frozen over during an extended cold spell. She was taken in by a white man living by the river, and he fed and sheltered her and the boy for a short time. He told her that the river was thawing and extremely dangerous and could not be crossed safely. When the man and Eliza heard dogs in the distance, they knew Eliza was being pursued, and she had to leave immediately. The white man who had sheltered her wrapped the baby in a woolen shawl and took a rail from his fence to give her some support should she break through the ice.[53] When she reached the river, she made her way from ice floe to ice floe to ice floe, sometimes falling, but saved from drowning by the rail. Exhausted, soaked with freezing water, she reached the Ohio side of the river at Ripley.[54] A slave catcher named Shaw, who often patrolled the river bank hoping to catch fugitives and claim a reward, unexpectedly helped her, perhaps because she had made such a perilous escape carrying a small child. He pointed out the home of John Rankin at the top of the hill. Rankin, a white Presbyterian minister, a long-standing abolitionist and Underground Railroad conductor, kept a lighted lantern in a window of his house, and many escaping slaves knew to walk toward that light and get help to reach Canada. Shaw reassured her: "No nigger was ever caught that got to his house."[55]

Late that night Eliza entered the Rankin house without knocking and was poking up the fire when Mrs. Rankin, hearing the noise, came into the kitchen and began to provide the fugitives with dry clothes

3. Josiah Henson and Eliza Harris

and food. Eliza put on one of Mrs. Rankin's linsey-woolsey dresses and the Rev. Rankin's socks. Her wet clothes and her son's were set out to dry at the fire. The Rev. Rankin arose and called two of his sons, John and Calvin. The boys knew that a long walk was in store for them, for escapees who arrived at the Rankin home needed to be moved to an underground railroad station away from Kentucky and the pursuers of the slaves as soon as possible.

John and Calvin, who was carrying the baby, walked the two late-night visitors to the home of a Scotch Presbyterian minister at Red Oak Chapel, five miles away. The Rankin boys then walked back home.[56] In his much later account of the incident, John Jr. wrote: "So far as we were concerned it was only another incident of many of a similar character. Strange how this unknown fugitive mother figured into the history of this country. She had no name, no monument erected to her. We two boys had helped to make history and were deaf, dumb and blind to its magnificence."[57]

The escaped slave woman and her son were moved from underground station to underground station, including one stop with a Quaker farm family near Sardinia, Ohio, and then on to the home of the Quaker businessman and abolitionist, Levi Coffin in Newport (now Fountain City), Indiana. She stayed there for several days, and Mrs. Coffin gave her the name Eliza Harris; information about the woman's safe arrival and her new name was likely sent back to the Rev. Rankin. Coffin then put Eliza Harris and son (his actual or assumed name has not come down to us) on the underground road to Sandusky, Ohio, where she crossed into Canada and settled in Chatham, Canada West.[58]

Perhaps the next year after Eliza crossed the river on the ice cakes, the Rev. Rankin related the story to the then unmarried Harriet Beecher. He probably told her that Eliza had been sent on to two Quaker conductors, but he would not have uses any names, including the Presbyterian minister who was the second conductor to help her. Those who aided escaping slaves faced legal penalties and needed to be anonymous. Rankin's story to Beecher would have ended with Eliza arriving in Canada. Rankin knew no more, and Beecher, soon married to Professor Stowe, was left with many opportunities to fictionalize Eliza and her story.[59]

Stowe uses Eliza's dramatic escape early in *Uncle Tom's Cabin* and then follows Eliza and her husband to Canada, Paris, and the planned trip to Africa, making many changes as she plots the story. In the novel, Stowe describes Eliza as a mulatto, slim, about 25, though the real Eliza was considerably older and had grandchildren, and was not slim. The real Eliza's son was two, not four as in the novel, and Stowe made this useful change to allow the child to talk, sing, and dance, giving him a strong personality.

In Stowe's fiction, Eliza does not go to the home of the Rankins, for Stowe had to protect the identity of the minister and his family. She has Eliza appearing at the home of a state senator named Bird, who like most politicians at the time was supporting anti-abolition activities. His wife, though, has great sympathy for Eliza and her son, now named Harry, and she is characterized as a near-perfect Christian woman. Stowe shows the senator quickly and amazingly turning from a shallow-thinking politician to a man of conscience ready to help Eliza escape. Stowe, whose own small son had recently died, then adds an emotional scene as Mrs. Bird goes through items of clothing once used by a now-dead small son and gives them to Harry.[60]

Senator Bird then spirits Eliza and Harry away to John Van Trompe, formerly a slave-holder in Kentucky who freed the men and women on his plantation and moved to the free state of Ohio. Stowe seemingly makes a bow to Rankin by having Van Trompe the father of seven strapping sons, all ready with their father to protect Eliza and Harry.[61] Stowe had been in the Rankin home and knew that the Rankins had many sons (eventually nine in all) who aided their mother and father in underground railroad activities. The Rankins, like the fictional Van Trompes, owned arms and were willing to use force when necessary.

Van Trompe then delivers the fugitives to a Quaker farm family, Simeon and Rachel Halliday and their several children.[62] Levi Coffin's friends thought the Hallidays were based on the Coffins, but that seems not to be true. When the Rev. Rankin told the story to Harriet Beecher, he would not have divulged the name of Coffin as one of the abolitionists who sheltered her. Stowe writes a generic picture of a Quaker abolitionist family, and she is effective in depicting such a family's belief in nonviolence in a violent world.

3. Josiah Henson and Eliza Harris

The reliable accounts about Eliza do not mention her husband, but in Stowe's fiction her hot tempered husband George had been so brutalized in slavery that he developed plans to flee. Though the two escaped at different times, they were reunited at the Halliday farm. Stowe also introduces Phineas Fletcher, a Quaker convert who married into the faith. He had rather unorthodox views, and he was not quite a convert to non-violence. Phineas had heard that a posse was going to capture Eliza, Harry, and George, and turn them over to the slave trader who had purchased them. George was armed with pistols, but Halliday, true to his Quaker beliefs, says to George, "be not over hasty with these — young blood is hot."[63] George responds that he wanted to be left alone, but if need be he would fight until death to save his wife and child. Stowe had found in her research about escaping slaves that George's views and his statement were common among escapees.

Though Eliza's husband George is a fictional creation, it is a useful one. He is an activist willing to fight for his freedom, in contrast to the passive Uncle Tom in the novel. Stowe also shows that George and Eliza wanted a stable married life, even though that institution was not recognized as valid for slaves.

Other fugitive slaves arrived at the Halliday home, and they all needed to be moved on toward Canada. The party of escapees left after dark, Phineas driving the covered wagon, a guard riding behind. The lookout spotted a posse of eight or ten liquored-up men riding hell-bent to capture the slaves and claim the reward money. Phineas pushed his horses as fast as they could go, the posse gained on the wagon. When Phineas came to an outcropping of rocks, he halted the wagon and all sought shelter. George and Jim, a new arrival at the Halliday farm, drew their pistols.

Stowe wants to show George as a man of courage willing to fight for his freedom, but his language is stilted as he calls out to a posse member who demands that the refugees surrender. "I am George Harris. A Mr. Harris, of Kentucky, did call me his property. But now I'm a free man, standing on God's free soil; and my wife and my child I claim as mine. Jim and his mother are here. We have arms to defend ourselves, and we mean to do it."[64]

In the gun battle that followed, George shot one of the posse members, Tom Loker. Tom was soon abandoned on the field of battle by his fellow slave-catchers who were outgunned by George and Jim. Tom was then taken to a nearby Quaker's home, where he was nursed back to health.[65] Stowe is historically correct when she praises Quakers for the work many of them did in opposing slavery and for the compassion they showed for people in need. George and Eliza were smuggled to Sandusky, Ohio, with Eliza dressed as a man and Harry as a little girl brought along by an "aunt." George arrived, and the Harrises settled in Amherstburg, Canada West.

Five years later, in Stowe's account, the Harrises had moved on to Montreal, where George supported his family as a machinist. Again, Stowe is historically correct, for skilled black craftsmen were in demand in Canada. Harry was in school and doing well. Eliza, "her form a little fuller,"[66] now had a daughter. Plot driven, Stowe has George miraculously reunited with his long-lost sister, now a wealthy widow, and Eliza with her mother, who had been Simon Legree's concubine.[67] Stowe departed from realism in this section.

Stowe's fictional family then sailed to France, where George attended a university for four years. When political troubles came to that country, they all returned to the United States. All were of a light color and could pass for white, but George did not wish to "identify" himself as American. Instead, he wanted to cast his lot with the oppressed in Africa as a teacher of Christianity. The extended Harris family sailed for Africa. In this ending, Stowe is gingerly supporting the "back to Africa" movement, opposed by most abolitionists and black and praised by southern slave holders who looked forward to shipping off troublemakers, especially free blacks, to Africa. Stowe does not fall into the slave-owners camp. She has George going there "As a Christian patriot, as a teacher of Christianity, I go to *my country*."[68] By sending the Harrises out of the country and to Africa Stowe shows that she could not envision an integrated society in the United States.

What Stowe did not know when she was gathering materials for her novel was that Eliza returned to see the Rankins in early July 1841, approaching the family as they worked in their vegetable garden. Eliza, a stout woman, was dressed as a man in pants and a waistcoat. "Oh,

3. Josiah Henson and Eliza Harris

Mister Rankin, I want my daughter and her children," she said. She was accompanied by a French-Canadian man she met in Cleveland, Ohio, who was going to help rescue her daughter and seven grandchildren owned by Thomas Davis in Dover, Kentucky.[69]

The Rev. Rankin warned the two visitors that she was likely to be captured and sold down the river, and he would be sentenced to be hanged. Eliza could not to be dissuaded, and her companion did not waver. He spoke English without an accent and was to get a job with the daughter's owner in Kentucky and make arrangements for a getaway. Eliza was to work on a nearby farm in Ohio to await the rescue. Mrs. Rankin made Eliza an appropriate dress to wear at the farm.

Jobs were plentiful that summer in Ohio and Kentucky, and Eliza and the French-Canadian were able to secure the jobs they needed to work out their plan.[70] By the first week in August, on Saturday night, they were ready to begin the rescue. The Rev. Rankin contributed two sons to the project—Samuel, 18, and John, 15. The boys each rode a horse, and they led one for Eliza to ride once they reached the farm where she had been working. They found the middle-aged, portly Eliza, a few inches over five feet tall, dressed as a man, waiting for them. Because the clothes she was wearing came from a corpulent man, she was wearing her own clothes underneath in order to fill them out. John remembered that she was a comical figure, but all knew that the mission was a dangerous one. Taking a little-traveled path, on that clear and starry night the Rankin boys and Eliza rode to the bank of the Ohio River, where they net the French-Canadian and Thomas Collins, a Ripley abolitionist who often worked with the Rankin family in helping escaping slaves.[71]

Collins was to return the three horses to the Rankin barn, and the French-Canadian and the two boys were to row the skiff over to the Kentucky shore, with Eliza as passenger. The trip had to be quiet, "not a splash, not a ruffle," John Jr. wrote, for it was imperative that the Kentuckians not be alerted to a plot to steal slaves.[72] The scene is reminiscent of Huck Finn and Jim on the Mississippi, with Jim fleeing for freedom and dreaming of stealing his family, and with danger on both banks of the river.

Once the four people reached Kentucky the boys quickly rowed back to Ripley, and Eliza and her companion were to go to the cabin of Eliza's daughter and help her and the children reach the river and then take a skiff back across to Ripley.

The plan quickly went awry, for Eliza and the French-Canadian did not take control as they should have. Eliza's daughter had packed up her possessions — two or three hundred pounds of them — and insisted on taking them along. Harriet Tubman, the black woman conductor, was an authoritarian when it came to her work in guiding escaping slaves. She would have forced the daughter to abandon all the bags, for the group of six children and three adults was in grave danger and needed to get to the river quickly. Instead, Eliza and her companion moved toward the river helping carry the possessions and the youngest child, 16 months old. Progress was slow, and it became clear they could not reach the river before dawn. They could not take a skiff in broad daylight to safety in Ohio.

The party hid in a heavily-wooded area to await the next night. One other part of the escape plan failed: the eldest of Eliza's grandchildren was in the main house the night of the escape and had to be left behind,[73] no doubt causing great emotional stress to Eliza and her daughter. Almost all the black refugees who reached Canada had to leave relatives behind, and the yearning to be reunited with families and friends was a major reason blacks left Canada at the end of the Civil War.

The French-Canadian executed a decoy plan. He took a skiff belonging to a pro-slavery man living near the Kentucky shore and rowed over to Rankin, leaving the skiff in plain sight. He reasoned that Mr. Davis, the owner of the slaves, and the posse he was certain to hire, would think the fugitives were somewhere in Ripley and spend Sunday searching for them there. That was exactly what happened.[74]

By the time the Rankins left church that Sunday morning a dozen horsemen were riding through Ripley, making their searches, but the escapees were not to be found. Whiskey was cheap in Ripley, and by midnight most members of the posse were drunk.

At 3 A.M. the next Monday morning the French-Canadian, Collins, and the Deacon of the Associate Reform Church went down to the river where Collins's skiff was tied up. Two men waited in the shad-

3. Josiah Henson and Eliza Harris

ows while the French-Canadian rowed across, picked up the fugitives, and within two hours returned to Ripley. According to Ann Hagedorn's brilliant account of this episode in *Beyond the River*, based on versions written by the Rev. Rankin's sons, Eliza then produced a small bag of gold coins to pay the French-Canadian, and he disappeared.[75] Where did she get the money? From working as a cook or washerwoman in Canada? Or did she find some generous person or church wanting to assist her in retrieving members of her family?

Collins and the Deacon were left to get the escapees to a safe house in Rankin, an attic room in the residence of Thomas McCague, the wealthiest businessman in that area and one not known to the public for his abolitionist activities. On Monday morning, McCague left on his business rounds, but he sent a message to the Rev. Rankin that the fugitives were safe in the McCague attic. Mrs. McCague took food and clothing to the guests hidden in her house, and Rankin had to make new plans for the escapees to get on the Underground Railroad. Originally, the plan was to have them taken to the nearby farm where Eliza had been working. A friend had loaned a wagon for the Sunday escape, but since Eliza and her family were delayed, the wagon had been returned.[76]

Meanwhile, members of the Davis posse, having slept off their corn liquor dreams, again rode through the Ripley streets looking for the fugitives. Another plan had to be put in place. Eliza and company had to be moved quickly and before dark to the hilltop home of the Rankins. John Jr. was the Rankin son who was to be the guide, along with two of his schoolmates whose parents were abolitionists. They were joined by the adult son of the founder of Ripley and by a local abolitionist couple. Mrs. McCague dressed the black baby in her daughter's clothes and carried her undetected, on horseback, to the farm where all the Harris family was to be brought. The three adults then individually escorted a fugitive to a spot where John Jr. and his two classmates were stationed. The boys then guided the two black women and the five remaining children to the Rankin home. That night the three boys were the guides taking the refugees to the farm where the baby was staying. A traveling salesman would take the eight runaways on to the next stop. Presumably the two or three hundred pounds of belongings were still with the Harris family. The boys returned to the Rankin home late at night, and the two friends stayed over with John Jr. They slept an hour or so, and then Mrs. Rankin had them up for breakfast and off to school. The boys were well-trained conductors. At school they were silent about their escapade,[77] which was more thrilling and dangerous than the romantic episodes dreamed up by Mark Twain's Tom Sawyer.

Eliza and her family returned to Chatham, Canada West, by way of Cleveland. The next decade must have been filled with hard work for Eliza and her daughter, for there were many children who needed support and care. We know nothing specific about their lives from 1841 when Eliza rescued her daughter and grandchildren until 1854 when Levi Coffin and his wife were visiting fugitives in Canada.

After a meeting at a black church, a woman came up to Mrs.

Left: Levi Coffin, a Quaker, was often called the President of the Underground Railroad (University of Illinois at Urbana-Champaign Library). Right: Catharine Coffin, a Quaker, helped feed and clothe the escaping slaves who came to their home before being sent on to Canada (University of Illinois at Urbana-Champaign Library).

3. Josiah Henson and Eliza Harris

Coffin, shook her hand, and exclaimed, "How are you, Aunt Kate? God bless you!" Mrs. Coffin did not recognize her at first, but the woman who had been called Eliza began recalling events at the Coffin home "in the days of her distress," and the Coffins then knew who she was. The Coffins visited her at her home and "found her comfortable and contented."[78]

Eliza now disappears from reliable sources. She is particularly hard to trace because we do not know the name she used when she was not on the run. In Canada, did she return to the name she used in slavery? Did she go on using "Eliza Harris?" Or did she choose an entirely different name?

There is one more sighting of Eliza, but it is highly questionable. In the last edition of his slave narrative, dated 1881, Joseph Henson wrote that Lewis G. Clarke, former slave and abolitionist activist, married Eliza and that they lived in Canada for a long time after their escape but finally moved to Oberlin, Ohio, to educate their children. In his old age, Henson's memory was unreliable, he did not write his books himself, and his ghost writer in 1881 (John Lobb) may have had a part in concocting this story about Eliza's later years.[79] Eliza and Clarke lived in different parts of Kentucky, and Clarke appears not to have had any contact with her in that state. He did not escape until 1841, three years after Eliza jumped from one ice black to another. He acted as an abolitionist activist and lecturer once he escaped and did not settle in Sandwich, Canada West, until 1850, 12 years after Eliza reached Canada.[80]

Henson and his ghost writer probably confused fact and fiction because Harriet Beecher Stowe met and interviewed Clarke, and in the *Key to Uncle Tom's Cabin* she asserted that she used him as a major model (along with Frederick Douglass) in crafting the character of George Harris, Eliza's fictional husband.[81] All evidence indicates that the real Eliza did not have a husband when she escaped from slavery.

Eliza's life in Canada is unfortunately lost to us. We know only what Levi Coffin tells us: she was "comfortable and contented," certainly an improvement over her existence in slavery.

4

Madison Washington

> I nestle in the mane of the British lion, protected by his mighty paw from the talons and the beak of the American eagle. I AM FREE, and breathe an atmosphere too pure for slaves, slave-hunters, or slave-holders.
>
> — Frederick Douglass' fictional
> Madison Washington in *The Heroic Slave*

The slave Madison Washington arrived in Canada in late 1839 or early 1840. According to a *Friend of Man* article reprinted in the *Liberator* on June 10, 1842, Washington was born in Virginia and "like the 'creole protestants,' "he was a very large and strong slave."[1] Just why Washington fled northward is not known, but harsh treatment is the reasonable supposition. He left behind a wife. Just how he reached Canada is not known, but it is likely that he had help from abolitionists because upon arriving in his new country, according to the *Friends of Man* article, "He staid awhile in the family of Hiram Wilson...."[2] Wilson was then working to help slaves in the area across the river from Detroit; that is, around Amherstburg and the Dawn settlement. Abolitionists often sent fugitive slaves to Wilson.

Since Wilson was particularly interested in education, he probably began to teach Washington to read and write. Washington stayed only a short time in Canada and it is unlikely that he was a homesteader. It is more likely that he did manual work for a white farmer or was employed as a logger in the forests.

Though Washington rejoiced in British liberty, "he loved his wife, who was left a slave in Virginia, still more."[3] In this love story the name of the beloved in unknown. How long they had been together is not recorded. There is every reason, however, to believe that the love of the two was genuine. The great affection slave men and women felt for their wives, husbands and children was a common theme in abolitionist stories about slavery and also in slave narratives.

Isaac Forman, a dark mulatto, then 23, wrote William Still after Still had sent him on to Toronto. Forman, allowed to see his wife only once or twice a year, escaped to Philadelphia in 1854, and after arriving in Canada wrote to his underground railroad conductor: "My soul is vexed, my troubles are inexpressible. I often feel as if I were willing to die. I must see my wife in short, if not, I will die." He was planning to leave Canada soon in an attempt to steal his wife. He blamed himself for escaping and leaving his wife behind. He lamented, just as Washington had done, "What is freedom to me, when I know my wife is in slavery?"[4]

Washington left Canada in 1841 and headed for Virginia, taking the Underground Railroad in reverse. He arrived at a station in Rochester, New York, operated by Lindley Murray Moore, a Quaker teacher. Moore collected money for him and gave the fugitive $10, suggesting Washington was traveling by public transportation.[5]

Washington was next in Utica, New York, being helped by the black minister Henry Highland Garnet who was opposed to nonviolence and urged slaves to arm themselves and rebel. Revolt is what Washington was later to do when he planned and put into successful operation the mutiny on the *Creole*. Garnet urged Washington not to return to Virginia, obviously because of the danger.[6]

Washington met in Pennsylvania with the wealthy black abolitionist Robert Purvis. Frederick Douglass, fascinated by Washington's story, later wrote his only fictional piece, "The Heroic Slave," which had an account of the fugitive directly from Purvis: Purvis urged Washington "not to go, and for a time he was inclined to listen to his counsel. He told him it would be of no use for him to go, for that as sure as he went he would only be himself enslaved, and could of course do nothing towards freeing his wife. Under the influence of his counsel he consented not to go; but when he left the house of Purvis, the thoughts of slavery came back to his mind to trouble his peace and disturbed his slumbers."[7] Washington left for Virginia.

Although several helping Washington gave him advice not to continue his quest to rescue his wife, not one of them had a practical plan to free Mrs. Washington. They could have raised money to employ a slave stealer, or they could have raised money to purchase her. They did neither of these things, and there is no indication they recognized just how much Washington loved his wife.

Washington did face greater danger in Virginia, was captured, and sold to the slave trader Thomas McCargo. The author of the *Friend of Man* article on Washington was undoubtedly correct: "And as it is the custom with slaveholders in more northern slave States to send the fugitive when received by them to the extreme South — lest he escape again — lest he communicate to other slaves the incidents of his day of freedom — as an example that shall strike terror to the breast of his fellows — he is sold to the southern market."[8]

Virginia then had an oversupply of slaves, and the deep southern states were expanding their agricultural areas and were in need of slave labor. New Orleans with their many slave pens, traders, and plantation owners was the preferred destination for internal slave ships. Madison Washington was put aboard the *Creole* in Richmond, Virginia, along with 134 slave men and women. The *Creole* sailed on October 25, 1841, and Washington was the slave cook. As he gave out food to his fellow slaves, he had an unique opportunity to speak to the blacks on board. He recruited 18 slave men to follow him in a mutiny, and they were aided by several of the black women. Moreover, Washington's efforts were helped by sexual tensions between blacks and whites on the ship. The black men prisoners were separated from the black women, and the black men were ordered not to enter the black women's quarters. Six black women, undoubtedly the most attractive in the group, were designated "maids" to carry out household duties for the white crew members; they were also "wives," serving the sexual needs of the crew.

On the night of November 7, 1841, the *Creole* was about 130 miles north of the Bahamian island of Abaco. In the early darkness, the Captain had ordered the brig laid to. The slaves had been sent to their quarters, the captain, accompanied by his family, passengers, and the crew, except for First Mate Gifford and guard William Merritt, had turned in for the night. Gifford was on watch at 9 P.M. when Elijah Mor-

4. Madison Washington

ris, one of the slave conspirators, shouted that a male slave had gone into the quarters housing the 40 or so slave women. Gifford called for Merritt, acting as guard in exchange for passage to New Orleans, to come help. Gifford called down to the women, who were part of the conspiracy, asking if men were there, and the women called out "Yes."

Gifford and Merritt knew what needed to be done. The sexual activities needed to be interrupted, the slave men whipped, and then returned to their quarters.

Merritt had an unlighted lamp in his hand, and Gifford gave him a match. Merritt descended into the women's quarters and could see Madison Washington. Merritt addressed the slave as "Doctor," a traditional title for black cooks: "Doctor, you are the last person I would expect to find here."

"Yes, sir, it is me," and he jumped on the deck, saying, "I am going up; I cannot stay here."[9]

Merritt and Gifford tried to catch him, but Merritt had a serious problem. He had a lighted lamp in his hand, and if he dropped it there was danger of fire. The deck was imperfectly lit from the lamp and from a lantern hanging in the bow. Washington ran forward and Morris appeared from the shadows, pistol in hand, and his shot grazed the back of Gifford's head.

Washington then shouted to his male co-conspirators: "Come up, every damned one of you: if you don't and lend a hand, I will kill you all and throw you overboard."[10]

17 slaves joined Washington and Morris, and in dramatic fashion they captured the *Creole*, with the loss of only one white man, and had the ship sailed into Nassau, where the British took control. We have an account of the entire mutiny and its aftermath in *The Creole Mutiny: A Tale of Revolt Aboard a Slave Ship*.

Most of the slaves were released almost immediately, but Washington and the male ring-leaders were held for a time because of the murder of a guard. Their captivity was not long. On April 16, 1843, the chief justice in Nassau addressed Washington and the mutineers: "It had pleased God to set you free from the bonds of slavery; may you hereafter lead the lives of good and faithful subjects of Her Majesty's

Government."[11] Had Washington sailed the *Creole* into a Canadian port, he would have heard the same words from a judge.

After liberating his wife in Virginia, Madison Washington undoubtedly planned for the two of them to proceed to Canada on the Underground Railroad. The British government would have recognized her as free, just as they had earlier accepted Madison Washington. She, however, remained in slavery and he was free in the Bahamas.

5

The Shadd Family

The Shadd family, with branches in the United States and Canada, descended from Hans Schadd, born in Kassel, Hesse, in 1725. He came to America in 1755 as a German mercenary soldier serving under British General Edward Braddock. During the run-up to the French and Indian Wars, Schadd was injured at Chadd's Ford. He was cared for by two free black women, Elizabeth Jackson and her daughter Elizabeth. Schadd married the daughter in 1756. The Schadds settled near Wilmington, Delaware, where he became a butcher. Elizabeth Schadd was proprietor of a successful tea room serving blacks and whites in Wilmington. The Schadds were hard-working and increasingly prosperous. Their son Jeremiah, born in 1758, was also a butcher, but he added shoemaking to his skills. Jeremiah Schad (the name was spelled various ways, including Shad, before Shadd became standard) married twice, both times to mulattoes, and fathered 15 children. According to family tradition, one of his wives was a refugee from Santo Domingo and had French manners. She, like her mother-in-law, was an astute businesswoman and had a food stand at a city market in Wilmington.

Abraham D. Shadd was born to Jeremiah and Amelia Shadd in 1801. A shoemaker, Abraham married Harriet Parnell, a mulatto from North Carolina, and they had 13 children. He was an activist in various abolitionist activities. He took subscriptions for William Lloyd Garrison's *Liberator*, and he opposed the colonization plans to resettle blacks in Africa. In 1831 he was elected vice-president at the First Annual Convention of Free People of Color, and he served as president of the Convention for the Free People of Color in 1833. He supported the American Anti-Slavery Society and took part in Underground Railroad activities. From his surviving letters, it is clear that he was an articulate and thoughtful man, a believer in education, hard work, and thrift.

Mary Ann, born in 1823, was the first of Abraham D. and Harriet's 13 children. Because there were no appropriate schools for black children in Wilmington, in 1833 Shadd moved his family to West Chester, Pennsylvania, where there were schools for the children. Mary Ann, who was to be an activist as her father was, probably attended a Quaker school. Abraham prospered as a shoemaker, and within a few years he also purchased a farm. The Shadd family was not wealthy, but they lived comfortably.

At the age of 16, Mary Ann left school and returned to Wilmington to teach free black children. She stayed there a few years but left when the educational opportunities for blacks improved. She then taught in various cities in free states.[1]

After the Fugitive Slave Act of 1850 was passed, large numbers of fugitives and free blacks left the United States for Canada, where they would have the protection of the law. Teachers were especially needed. Mary Ann went to Toronto in September of 1851 to attend a meeting concerning the hated fugitive law and the possibilities for blacks to immigrate to the northern country. Some of those in attendance probably knew Mary Ann's father, for he had been active in abolitionist circles for two decades. There she met Henry Bibb, one of the organizers of the conference, and he encouraged her to remain and teach in the western part of Canada West.

Mary Ann found that proposal intriguing. She possessed a pioneer spirit with its emphasis on self-help, self-reliance, and entrepreneurship. She wrote one of her brothers, probably Isaac, on September 16, 1851, as she was leaving Toronto for Sandwich in Canada West, that if he emigrated, shoemaking paid well and he should work at his craft and buy land with the money he made. She urged him to "be particular about company — be polite to every body — go to church, every body does to be respected." She recommended that he attend integrated churches on a regular basis and black churches occasionally. She also suggested that he should board at an integrated house.[2] Integration was her long-term goal, a cause she fought for during her years in Canada. She was idealistic when she wrote her brother, declaring

5. The Shadd Family

that everyone was respected according to his ability. She was soon to learn about racial discrimination in Canada.

Encouraged by Bibb, Mary Ann moved to Windsor, Canada West, across the river from Detroit. She found the village crowded with destitute escaped slaves and an often hostile white population. Housing for blacks was inadequate, and there was no school for black children or for their parents who wanted to learn to read and write. At first she was helped by the already-established Henry Bibb.

Bibb was born in Shelby County, Kentucky, in 1815 to a white father and a slave mother. From an early age, he was determined to be free. Openly discontented, he was often sold, and finally in 1841 he was able to escape. During his previous escape attempts, he had tried to contact and rescue his slave wife and daughter, but all these efforts had failed. Once he learned in 1845 that his wife Malinda was now the concubine of her owner, he declared that she "had finally given me up."[3] Bibb blamed the victim, not the system of slavery itself, and his attack on Malinda seems self-serving.

Bibb felt free to marry again, and this time he chose a Boston lady, Mary Miles, a teacher who was a supporter of anti-slavery causes. The Bibbs had moved to Sandwich, Canada West, and in 1851 Bibb established a newspaper, *The Voice of the Fugitive*. Mary Bibb was conducting a private school in Sandwich. Mary Ann Shadd, recognizing the possibility of friction should she begin a school in Windsor, discussed the matter with Mary Bibb. Mrs. Bibb was agreeable, but the Bibbs and Shadd were strong-minded and were soon to clash over many issues.

According to Canadian law, blacks could enroll their children in public schools, but white parents were often opposed and black children were ostracized. Blacks could also petition to have all-black schools, but the legal steps were complicated enough to ensure that some blacks had no school at all. A segregated black school was being considered in Windsor; the Bibbs were for it and Shadd against it. Shadd made a counterproposal: If the plan for a segregated school would be abandoned, she would organize a private school for 20 students, open to all races, with a fee of three shillings a month for each pupil.[4]

Mary Ann Shadd resisted the advice of the Bibbs, and she soon opened an integrated private school with day and night classes. She had an unsatisfactory school room in an unused barracks building, with the AME Church also having services in part of the derelict building. Shadd's activities could be closely watched by church members. Though Shadd had been a member of the AME Church at one time, she refused to join the Windsor congregation because it was entirely black. Her stand on principle was much discussed and often deplored by members of the black religious community.

At first Mary Ann had 13 day students and 11 adults enrolled in night classes. She always had white students in attendance. She reported that the adults and children were anxious to learn, but many were unable to pay the small fee, and she knew of at least 25 children not attending class for that reason. Shadd then turned reluctantly to the American Missionary Association (AMA) for financial assistance. She had wanted to conduct a self-supporting school, but that was proving difficult because of the poverty of many of the refugees. She requested that the AMA provide her a salary of $250 a year, certainly reasonable in light of the average wage of $20 a month for black people in that area. The AMA offered half support ($125 a year), with the balance to be made up from her fees. Unfortunately, few could pay; in February of 1852 she received the equivalent of $2 for tuition. She accepted the AMA offer but did not mention that support to her clients because she feared all parents would then quit paying, thinking she did not need the money. She also feared that Mary Bibb might misunderstand and make misrepresentations about the grant.[5]

The Bibbs and Shadd had different philosophies about schools, especially the matter of segregated schools. In addition, Mary Bibb was also a talented teacher, though erratic in her personal life. Shadd charged the Bibb swore and took drugs.[6] Others in the community noted her irregular behavior, which might have been caused by drug use. The three continually squabbled over the Refugee Home Society which proposed to purchase 50,000 acres of land in Canada and establish a fugitive slave community. To do so, money had to be raised outside of Canada, and this fund raising quickly became "begging." Bibb was one of the prime movers in the Refugee Home Society, but it was

5. The Shadd Family

badly mismanaged, and there were charges that funds were routinely used by the Bibbs for their personal use. Shadd believed strongly in integration and recommended that blacks should take up government land rather than be confined into segregated colonies. The Bibbs had a newspaper which often printed charges against Shadd, but she had to depend on conversations with local citizens, public addresses, and letters to the editor to make her case. She charged that Bibb had been given Bibles for distribution but that he refused to give any of them to Shadd for school use. She insisted that Bibb had large quantities of clothes to give out to indigent fugitives, clothes contributed in the United States as a result of "begging," but that he refused to distribute them to the poor. Bibb continued his attacks on Shadd, charging falsely that she would not accept white students in her school. He also discovered and published the story of her secretly accepting $125 from the AMA, forcing Shadd to admit the truth of the accusation and attempt to justify her action.[7]

In 1852 Shadd wrote a well-received pamphlet urging blacks to come to Canada, the land of freedom.[8] Her parents had been considering leaving the United States, and in the summer of that same year her father Abraham came north to investigate the advisability of moving his family from Pennsylvania "to settle in the Queen's Free Soil." Before the end of the year, he purchased two plots of land outside North Buxton and near the Elgin Settlement. He probably did not move until early spring the next year, and, unlike many fugitives who walked to Canada, he and his family undoubtedly came by "real" train as opposed to underground train, bringing with them their personal goods and the tools of the shoemaking trade. The Shadds were a close-knit family, and their long involvement in abolitionist activities certainly gave Mary Ann credibility and helped her in the ongoing disputes with the Bibbs.

Mary Ann also kept busy with her teaching duties, which included night classes and Sabbath day instruction. This was her schedule in 1852 for her week-day classes, giving us an idea about the scope of her teaching in a one-room school:

2 classes in Geography
1 class in History

1 class in Colburn's arithmetic
2 classes in Grammar
1 class in 3rd Reader
1 class in 2nd Reader
1 class in Written Arithmetic
1 class in Botany.[9]

Her weekday school was solidly academic and clearly not steeped in religion, though she probably had students reading religious stories.

By all accounts, Shadd was a creative teacher, but the AMA, fearful of controversy, withdrew its $125 stipend a year for her, apparently believing that her religious views were not sound and that some of the charges against her being made by the Bibbs might be true. The Bibbs and AMA officials had difficulty dealing with the strong-willed, independent Shadd, who never hesitated to speak her mind.

Without financial support and subjected to continued attack in the Bibbs' newspaper, Shadd decided to leave teaching. She was disgusted with her situation and wanted to change. She left Windsor for Toronto for a time and began to make plans to publish her own newspaper, *The Provincial Freeman*, to be written for blacks in Canada. She was soon joined by her brother Isaac who helped with editorial work. The paper appeared on March 25, 1853, with the motto: "Self-reliance is the True Road to Independence." The goal of the paper was to "represent the 40,000 Negroes, freedom, fugitives, wealthy and poor" newly arrived in Canada. The paper was committed to ending discrimination against blacks and encouraging integration and educational and cultural opportunities.[10]

Bibb's paper, *The Voice of the Fugitive*, published from Sandwich, had first appeared two years earlier, and it, too, served the needs of black people in Canada. Bibb did excellent interviews with recently-arrived fugitives, gave information which allowed those new to Canada to find family members and friends. Bibb supported the land colonies and the practice of "begging" for funds to purchase land. Shadd was adamantly opposed to his approach to assisting fugitives. Both editors uses intemperate language in arguing their cases and both made uncalled-for personal attacks.[11] The black population in Canada could

5. The Shadd Family

not support two newspapers, and both ceased publication; Bibb's paper did not long survive his premature death in 1854. Shadd's paper lasted only a few more years.

During her newspaper years, Shadd married Thomas Cary, a black barber, and had two children, Sarah and Linton. She became more radical in the years just before the Civil War began. John Brown, planning his attack upon slavery, came to Chatham, Canada West, in the spring of 1858 and was supported by the Shadd family, Mary Ann's husband, and some of their friends. One of Brown's followers was Osborne P. Anderson, who had come to Canada when Mary Ann's uncle Absalom had settled near her father's farm. Anderson had become a printer's devil and assistant at the *Provincial Freeman*. Brown is said to have stayed with Isaac Shadd during this visit to Canada, and the Shadds and other local supporters were aware of the nature of Brown's planned attack on the institution of slavery. Mary Ann later said that had she been a man, she would have ridden with Brown. Anderson was the only Canadian black to fight with Brown at Harpers Ferry. He survived, returned home, and in 1861 published his account of the episode, called *A Voice from Harpers Ferry*, which was edited by Mary Ann.

Many in the United States and Canada who knew John Brown's plans were frightened after his failed raid and denied any involvement. Shadd was not silent. She knew his plans for the Harpers Ferry attack because he trusted her and members of her family. She completely approved of his kind of abolitionism.[12]

Thomas Cary died in 1860, and Mary Ann and her children were poverty-stricken. Her newspaper was no longer published on a regular basis. She had to look for help from her family, many of whom were well off. Her father had established a profitable farm near North Buxton. Highly regarded in the community, he was elected to the Raleigh Town Council in 1859. Mary Ann found it hard to depend on others for money.

Mary Ann's financial troubles continued during the early years of the Civil War, but in 1863 Dr. Martin Delany came to her aid. Delany, a free black, had studied medicine with a white physician in Pittsburgh. In 1850 he was admitted to the Harvard Medical School, but white students protested and he was dismissed. He assumed the title of Dr. and was in medical practice in Chatham, Canada West, in 1856. He was a friend of the Shadd family and a supporter of John Brown. When the war began, he went to Washington to offer his services as a recruiting officer but was rejected because of his connections with John Brown and the raid at Harpers Ferry. Delany appealed directly to Lincoln, who then recommended that Delany be given a commission as a major. Delany then began to seek black volunteers in Chatham. His and others' recruiting drives for the Union army were successful: 700 blacks may have enlisted from Buxton alone.

Delany set about organizing the 104th Regiment of Colored Troops as the war was ending. Abraham W. Shadd, Mary Ann's brother, was brought in as captain of the newly-established regiment.[13]

Earlier, Dr. Delany in December 1863 had written Mary Ann that he would pay her $15 for each black man she recruited. This recruiting opportunity was of special importance to her. Over the years, Mary Ann had grown increasingly concerned about the racist climate in Canada West. She wanted to be able to support her children, and she wanted to aid the war effort and bring about the end of slavery. She left Canada and began recruiting in Indiana with success. The black activist William Wells Brown wrote that her recruits were carefully chosen.

At the end of the war Shadd joined the large number of blacks permanently leaving Canada. For a time, she taught in Detroit, not far from her father and other relatives who remained in Canada. In 1869 she moved to Washington, D.C., where she worked as teacher and school principal. She also studied law at night at Howard University, enrolling in the two-year program. She should have graduated with the class of 1871 but did not, perhaps because of her heavy teaching and administrative work. Her brother Abraham W. did graduate in law that year and moved to Mississippi, where he entered politics. Years later, Mary Ann reentered the Howard University law school and received a degree in 1883 when she was 60. She then began a law practice largely serving the black community.

In addition to her new career as an attorney, Shadd continued to work for women's rights and women's suffrage, and she never gave up speaking against racial discrimination. She died in 1893, leaving an estate of $150. She was a dedicated, assertive anti-segregationist, a battler for equal rights for women.[14]

Some Shadds remained in Canada, others returned to the United States after the war. Mary Ann's son worked as a messenger in the House of Representatives in Washington. Her daughter took classes at Howard University. Her brother Isaac moved to Mississippi in 1870 and at first worked as a bookkeeper for B.T. Montgomery & Sons, former slaves who were growing what was called the best cotton in the state on property previously owned by Jefferson Davis's brother. Isaac was elected speaker of the Mississippi House of Representatives in 1872. Her brother Abraham was an attorney in that state. Her father continued to live in North Buxton until his death in 1881. Her brother Garrison was a well-to-do farmer in Kent County, Canada West. Her brother Alfred and sister Emaline were teachers, he at the highly-regarded Buxton Mission School and she at schools in Canada and at Howard University.[15]

Mary Ann Shadd Cary's cousin Furman Jeremiah Shadd, son of Absalom Shadd, was born in Washington, D.C., in 1852, about three years before Absalom sold his profitable hotel-restaurant business and moved to Chatham, Canada West, to live on a farm near his brother, Abraham D. Shadd. After Absalom's death, the family returned to Washington, and young Shadd entered the Howard University prep school. He later received his B.S. degree in 1875, was valedictorian of his class, and completed his M.S. in 1878. His medical degree was granted in 1881, and again he was the first in his class. Like Mary Ann, he was also a teacher, and during his student days at Howard he served as tutor in math at the university's normal school before he became assistant principal and then principal from 1879 until 1881. After graduation from medical school, he was appointed assistant surgeon and resident at Freedmen's Hospital, the teaching facility of the Howard Medical School. He also taught in the medical school and was appointed full professor in 1891. That same year, Dr. Shadd applied to the local American Medical Association for membership and was rejected because of his race. Although spurned by the white medical establishment, he clearly made the best of opportunities available to him. When Dr. Rudolph Virchow, the famous German pathologist, was in the United States in 1893, Dr. Shadd met with him. Dr. Shadd studied in Europe in 1906 and conferred with the German bacteriologist Dr. Robert Koch, who discovered the organisms causing anthrax, tuberculosis, Asiatic cholera, and other diseases. Dr. Koch had received the Nobel Prize in Physiology and Medicine in 1905.

Dr. Shadd was a respected physician and medical school teacher and was also involved for many years in organizations that benefited the political, cultural, and social lives of blacks. Though he and Mary Ann Shadd Cary were of different generations, they undoubtedly worked together on various programs during the years they lived in the District of Columbia. Dr. Shadd died in 1908.[16]

Mary Ann's nephew Dr. Alfred Schmitz Shadd is another impressive member of that family. His grandfather was Abraham Dorcas and his father Garrison Shadd. He was born in 1870 near Chatham and attended local schools. His father was a successful farmer, and the family was prominent in the community. He enrolled in the medical school of the University of Toronto and carried on the family tradition of claiming his rights by refusing to be a second-class citizen. Some white students in medical school refused to sit by him. He gave them choices: they could sit by him or fight him. As the photograph of him at about age 20 shows, he was a large young man. There were no fights. In 1896 he took a year off from his studies to teach children of homesteaders in Kinistino in the Carrot River Valley, Northwest Territories, now Saskatchewan. It is likely that he went to the remote Carrot Valley to determine if he could live the life of a free man and physician there, without racial prejudice and without being segregated. Amazingly, he found a near-utopia.

There were 366 schools and 422 teachers in the Northwest Territories, Shadd apparently being the only black teacher. The white children were curious about this large black man, but they were not hostile. One little girl, sitting on his knee, moistened her finger and touched his cheek. He assured her that the color was permanent. He was known as a humorous and disciplined teacher and had a successful year. He then returned to Toronto and completed his medical studies in 1898. He was soon back in Kinistino where he helped build a two room log house. His office was named the "Chamber of Horrors" and his bed-

5. The Shadd Family

Alfred Schmitz Shadd, grandson of Abraham D. Shadd about 20 (center) with two brothers, Wm. Abram (left) and Charles (Buxton National Site & Museum).

room the "Chamber of Silence." When he performed surgery, the wife of the local postmaster served as his anesthetist.[17]

Most of the Native Americans in that neighborhood had never seen a black man before, but Dr. Shadd's willingness to serve their medical needs made him a favorite among the Cree Indians. Like many of his relatives, he sought to help disadvantaged people of color, but he also built a large white practice. In 1904 he moved to Melfort, the largest town in the Valley, where he continued to be available day or night to treat patients, whatever their ability to pay. Rain or snow would not impede the doctor. One resident remembered, "If there was no trail for the buggy or cutter he would take to horseback."[18] Once he reached the patient, he had world and enough time for the treatment. He was a gregarious man, known for his humor and compassion. He seems to have been completely accepted in the Valley and apparently did not suffer racial discrimination.

Dr. Shadd had the easy optimism and entrepreneurial spirit also found on the frontier of the United States. He owned a drugstore, helped establish a newspaper and wrote editorials for it. In the fertile valley where hard wheat was a major crop, he established a mixed farm, raising fruit, hogs, and prize cattle. He was a believer in scientific farming and paid $1,000 for a white bull to improve his herd. He would, when needed, also act as veterinarian: during one farm visit he delivered a baby and a calf.[19]

He was a solid citizen, supporting community development such as waterworks and sewers, the planting of trees, and the beautification of the town. At the same time this handsome man was a dramatic figure in this isolated area. In 1906 he bought a red Reo when cars came to the Valley, and he was known as a speed demon when he made his rounds to see patient and to supervise his farm.[20]

Dr. Shadd was one of the founders of Lady Minto Hospital in Melfort. He was involved in the details of its planning and operation, and he was not reluctant to speak his mind to the directors of the hospital. When they raised the daily rates for the hospital, he argued that the fees were too high. He wanted hospital funds used for a good cause and urged the purchase and equipping of an ambulance. He scolded the superintendent of nurses for allowing smoking in the wards. He

5. The Shadd Family

was interested in improving his medical skills and took a six months sabbatical in 1904 to study in Edinburgh and Paris, something few frontier doctors were able to do.[21]

He ran for a seat in the Northwest Territories Assembly. He was for a stronger provincial government, for internal improvements such as railroad construction, and he favored provincial control of public lands. Like his aunt Mary Ann, he was concerned that schools should not be segregated. He called for local control of schools and for a curriculum that would bring about "good Canadian citizens of incoming races and creeds."[22] He was narrowly defeated in the election.

Dr. Shadd was a loyal Canadian, with ties going back to the government which gave legal protection to thousands of blacks who fled the United States. He was a warden in the Anglican church and paid for the bells when the church was built in 1906. He was married in that church to a white woman, and there was no public outcry about race mixing. The couple had two children, a boy and girl.[23]

Dr. Shadd died in 1915 from acute appendicitis. The newspaper accounts of his funeral make no mention of his race. He and his children were the only blacks in the community, and he had become a respected member of Valley life. Native Americans were discriminated against, but Dr. Shadd had a special

Dr. Alfred Schmitz Shadd had a successful career as a physician in Saskatchewan (Buxton National Site & Museum).

relationship with them. Indian friends felt "out of place"[24] at his funeral services in the church; they gathered at the cemetery to pay their respects to the man who had treated them as equals.

Dr. Shadd was obviously aware of racism in the United States and Canada, but he was in a Shangri-La in the Valley. Would Dr. Shadd have suffered racial discrimination had there been ten blacks in the Valley? One thousand? Perhaps, but given his personality, he would not have meekly accepted second class citizenship. Perhaps his special circumstances—his decision to move to the frontier, his outgoing personality, his easy personal relationships, and his excellent medical training—allowed him to live in an integrated society, something Mary Ann Shadd Cary and Dr. Jeremiah Shadd could not do in the District of Columbia during and after Reconstruction.

From the time of Hans Schadd, the Shadds were a remarkable family both in the United States and Canada, public-spirited citizens committed to education and to the rights of minorities.

6

Lewis Richardson, Formerly a Slave on Henry Clay's Plantation

> The American Secretary of State, Henry Clay, who was a slave-owner, resented the readiness of Upper Canada to accept escaped slaves. He declared this policy a growing evil and several times asked Britain to order fugitive slaves returned, but with little success. British courts upheld the principle that "...every man is free who reaches British ground."
>
> — Hill, *The Freedom-Seekers*

Lewis Richardson, free at last, spoke to citizens of Amherstburg in Canada West on May 13, 1846. He was then 53 years old, and the last nine years of his life he had been a slave on Henry Clay's estate, Ashland. Richardson was addressing a friendly group in Canada, with many "cheers" from the audience. He began his talk in a way that ensured support of runaway slaves and praised the British government for welcoming fugitive slaves: "Dear Brethren, I am truly happy to meet with you on British soil (cheers,) where I am not know by the color of my skin, but where the Government knows me as a man."[1]

Richardson answered those who believed that slaves had rather live on Clay's estate than to be free: "I had rather this day have a millstone tied to my neck, and be sunk to the bottom of Detroit river, than to go back to Ashland and be a slave for life."[2]

Richardson escaped for two main reasons. The first was severe punishment he had received on Clay's estate. According to his dramatic speech, in December 1845 "Henry Clay had me stripped and tied up, and one hundred and fifty lashes given me on my naked back; the crime for which I was so abused was, I failed to return home on a visit to see my wife, on Monday morning before 5 o'clock."[3] His wife lived on another farm about three miles away. Slaves returning late from conjugal visits were often severely punished. Even if Richardson exaggerated the number of lashes he received, that punishment was cruel. Richardson believed he would not have survived at Ashland because Clay's overseer was disposed to giving out violent punishment. Richardson wanted to be free, even if it meant capture during flight and death.

The second reason Richardson wanted to escape from Ashland was the lack of adequate clothing and food there. According to Richardson, he was give no clothes in nine years, but did receive one "small course blanket."[4] Each field hand received a peck of roughly-ground corn and a small amount of meat each week, their diet disproving Clay's boast that his slaves were "fat and sleek."[5] Mistreatment had made Richardson flee, but he had to leave his wife behind, much to his regret.

Richardson did not give an account of his escape from Kentucky to Canada; to do so would have endangered those blacks and whites who had helped him. He expected to be pursued as a felon, but he fortunately eluded the bounty hunters and arrived on free soil. "Hail Britannia," he said, "Shame America! (Cheers)."[6] Now as free as Clay was when a candidate for the office of president of the United States, Richardson pointed stated that Clay "was running for slavery and I for liberty."[7]

The black newspaper editor Henry Bibb then spoke, hailing Richardson as a brother now enjoying in Canada those famous qualities spoken of in the Declaration of Independence: "life, liberty, and the pursuit of happiness."[8] Bibb then gave to fugitive slaves the same advice given to immigrants going to the frontier areas in the United States—work for yourselves on fertile land. With hard work, Richardson would be an example of former slaves who could take care of themselves. Bibb urged Richardson's motto to be honesty and integrity.[9]

The test of Richardson's speech and Bibb's response appeared in the *Anti-Slavery Bugle*, April 24, 1846. The article was probably written by Bibb, but there is no by-line. Pro-slavery response came quickly.

6. Lewis Richardson, Formerly a Slave on Henry Clay's Plantation

Five white men who knew Richardson when he was enslaved called him a "hard-drinking, insolent, obstreperous, unmanageable" slave who sold whiskey to his fellow slaves and fought whites and blacks alike.[10]

This joint statement of the five men attacking Richardson's character can not now be fairly evaluated, for the charges against him can not be verified. He was said to have a bad reputation: He tried to murder his second owner, escaped to Ohio, was captured and sold down the river to Louisiana. Soon after he arrived there, according to charges against him, he stabbed his overseer. Clay acquired him about 1836. Was Richardson a violent criminal with propensities for murder or a man who lashed out at the violence perpetrated against him by owners and overseers? The men defending Clay and attacking Richardson asserted that Clay was an "indulgent" master, but there were several escaping slaves from Ashland, indicating problems with living conditions and with the overseer and with Clay himself.[11]

By all accounts, Richardson was a slave difficult to manage and control. He had five owners before Clay bought him. Clay's overseer, Ambrose Barnett, wrote that he had "never known a worse negro."[12] Barnett wrote the Lexington *Observer and Reporter* denying Richardson's charges and remarked that the slave once struck him. His flogging of Richardson was for an "accumulation of faults" and was given with the help of another overseer. Barnett insisted that he gave out 16 lashes.[13]

Richardson's speech at Amherstburg indicates he was a rational man whose "crime" was that he wanted to be free. He may have exaggerated conditions at Ashland, for extreme stories would please, even titillate, his audience. He seems intelligent and resourceful. Could it be that he sold whiskey to save money for his escape? Slaves with funds had a better change to escape, for they could buy forged papers, food, transportation, and pay bribes as needed.

Unfortunately, Richardson's later history is not chronicled, and his life in his new country is unknown.

Henry Clay (1777–1854), had a complex attitude toward slaves and slavery. When Clay was Secretary of State during John Quincy Adams's administration, he attempted in 1827 to get the British to return slaves who had escaped to Canada. Hunting down these fugitives often led to difficulties. He argued that the escaped slaves were worthless and that the British government should send them back to their owners for the good of Canada. The British government refused.[14]

Over his long adult life, Clay believed and often declared that slavery was an evil institution. He saw a solution in the one offered by the American Colonization Society: return freed slaves to Africa. Most slaves and most abolitionists opposed this solution.

Clay's views on slavery were somewhat more progressive than many of his fellow plantation owners in the South. He believed that slaves would eventually be emancipated, but that day never arrived in his lifetime. He played no role in efforts to abolish slavery.

Clay had a working, profitable farm at Ashland. In 1831 he had 15 slaves, but this number increased to more than 50 within a few years. The number of slaves at Ashland varied during Clay's later life. The Clay family was often away from Kentucky, living in Washington D.C., and had to rely on overseers to manage the farm operation and the slaves. Many overseers throughout the South had the reputation of dealing harshly with slaves, whether on the orders of the owner, or because the overseers were courting favor by increasing profits, or because they enjoyed punishing their slave charges. Whatever Clay thought about emancipation sometime in the distant future, he went on using slave labor at Ashland. Richardson was fortunate to have escaped from Ashland and from Barnett, the overseer directly responsible to Henry Clay, senator and presidential aspirant.[15]

7

The Blackburns

Thornton Blackburn was born a slave in Maysville, Kentucky, in 1812. His owner, Robert Smith, a deputy sheriff, may have been the child's father.[1] At the age of three, Thornton was sold. His new owner, George Morton, took the boy from his mother and gave him to his nine-year-old grandson, George Morton Murphy.[2] George's father, William Murphy, was postmaster of Washington, Kentucky, and the family lived in an imposing home. Blackburn as a child was taught good manners and his speech was refined; he was not, however, taught to read and write. In the Murphy household he was taught another skill that he was later to use in Canada — the care of horses.[3]

George Morton Murphy died about 1824, and William Murphy left Washington to become postmaster of Maysville, Kentucky. Thornton was then apprenticed as a stonemason,[4] a trade he also used in freedom. That phase of Thornton's life was short, for he was soon sold to a physician, Dr. Gideon Brown, of Hardinsburg, Kentucky. Thornton, then about 14, had several duties useful to him later, helping with horses, serving meals, and working on the Brown farm. In Toronto, Thornton first worked as a waiter, later began a cab operation and housed his horses in his barn, and he and his wife maintained a large garden and orchard.

When Thornton was 17 or 18, Dr. Brown died. As the estate was being settled, the slave's value was set at $400.[5] Judge Oldham, executor of the Brown estate, decided to hire out Thornton by the year in Louisville. Thornton became a porter in the mercantile establishment of Charles Wurts and John Reinhard.[6] The well-spoken, good-looking young Thornton had many duties, including driving the wagon to the docks to pick up merchandise for the store.

Thornton was freer from white supervision than he had ever been. Louisville was an important port on the Ohio river, and he came into contact with leased-out slaves and free blacks. He undoubtedly became aware of the abolitionist movement and the possibility of fleeing across the river to Ohio, a free state, and then on to Canada.[7]

Thornton met and fell in love with another mulatto, the beautiful Ruthie, a nursemaid in the George Backus home, where she cared for two children. Her background is unclear, but she was later to say she was a Creole born in the West Indies. She was eight or nine years older than Thornton. The two were married in 1831.[8] They were almost immediately faced with the nightmare common to slaves. George Backus's wife and daughter died, soon followed by George himself. Ruthie would undoubtedly be sold down the river. Since she was a beautiful woman, she most likely would become the concubine of a planter or wealthy merchant.

Harriet Beecher Stowe in *Uncle Tom's Cabin* made it clear that beautiful women slaves were sexual objects. In that novel, Stowe wrote about Cassy, who was being offered for sale: "...they made me dress up, every day; and gentlemen used to come in and stand and smoke their cigars, and look at me, and ask questions, and debate my price."[9] Stowe was not telling the whole sordid story; men and women slaves were routinely undressed and carefully inspected. As scholar Walter Johnson observed, "As they went about their slave-market business, slaveholders mapped their own forbidden desires into slaves' bodies...." A slave woman "indecently '*examined*' in the presence of a dozen or fifteen brutal men" was subjected to "brutal remarks and licentious looks." It was clear that the "stated concern about the women's capacity for reproduction served as a public cover for a much more general interest in her naked body."[10]

Ruthie's life as a concubine would not be a long one. She was already approaching 30, and her beauty would fade in a few years. In *Uncle Tom's Cabin*, Cassy had been bought by the planter Simon Legree and had become his mistress. She lived with him for five years and was between 35 and 40 years old. Legree put her aside, and as she said, "And now, he's got a new one, — a young thing, only fifteen...."[11]

Both Blackburns were badly frightened about the danger Ruthie

7. The Blackburns

was in, and there was nothing legal that Thornton could do to keep her from being sold away. There was an illegal way out, however, and though it was dangerous, they could flee to a free state.

But how? Henry "Box" Brown entered a coffin-like box and had himself shipped to Philadelphia.[12] They could, like Eliza, cross the Ohio River on the ice floes, but the Blackburns needed to escape in the summer. They might purloin a canoe or raft, cross the river in the dead of night, and start for Canada, perhaps getting help along the way from abolitionists and sympathetic underground railroad conductors. They could use disguises as Ellen and William Craft did. She dressed as an ill young planter going north for medical treatment, attended by her faithful slave, William.[13]

The Blackburns procured papers showing each to be free. Such papers could be purchased or they might be written by someone concerned about their plight. They then dressed carefully for their escape. According to the fugitive slave advertisement which appeared just days after their escape from Kentucky, Thornton, at 19, was five foot nine or ten, "stout made, and of a yellow complexion, light eyes, and of good address, had on when he left a blue cloth coat, pantaloons, boots, and a black hat."[14] Ruthie was dressed sedately in a black silk dress. The handsome couple appeared on July 3, 1831, at a ferry dock for transport to Indiana. The ferryman inspected their papers, and finding nothing wrong, he took them across. They had come to the conclusion that their passage on a riverboat would be improved if they were departing from the free state of Indiana. They waved to the passing *Versailles*, then departing Louisville for Cincinnati. The Captain took them aboard, examined their papers, and was satisfied with them. Because of her looks, Ruthie made more of an impression on the Captain and the crew than Thornton did. Both Blackburns would have been nervous and excited on the *Versailles*, fearing exposure all the time they were on the steamboat.[15]

Once the couple reached Cincinnati, they were still in danger, this time from the many slave catchers seeking bounties from the owners of escaped slaves. The Blackburns took passage on the mail stage coach, destination Sandusky, Ohio. They arrived there safely and took another coach to Detroit.

Arriving in Detroit, they went to the home of James Slaughter, a black man they met on the mail coach originating in Sandusky. The Blackburns stayed with him and his family for a short time. What they did not know was that he was an untrustworthy co-owner of a brothel.[16]

In hindsight, it is clear that the Blackburns should have gone on to Canada, just across the river from Detroit. In Canada they would be safe. Just why they stopped in Detroit is unclear. Perhaps abolitionists who helped them spoke highly of Detroit. Perhaps they had some fear of a foreign country. Instead, Thornton found work as a stonemason, and the two lived quietly for two years. Then there was an incident that should have sent them fleeing across the river for safety.

On a city street, Thornton was seen by Thomas Rogers, formerly a clerk in the Louisville firm where Thornton worked before his escape. The two talked cordially for a time. Thornton apparently claimed that he and Ruthie had been freed before they left Kentucky. Rogers eventually returned to Louisville and told about his meeting with Thornton. The owners of the two slaves wanted them back and began legal proceedings. On June 14, 1833, the 21-year-old Thornton was arrested and jailed. His owners, the estate of Dr. Brown, were using the provisions of the Fugitive Slave Law of 1793, which called for the return of runaway slaves to their rightful owners.[17]

At first, there was some question about Ruthie's slave status, but she was arrested on June 15, 1833. The black community was inflamed by these jailings, for there was real danger that these two well-liked Detroit residents might be sent back into slavery in Kentucky.

When the trial began, men and women crowded into the balcony and were noisy in their unhappiness at the proceedings. Some blacks threatened to burn Detroit unless the Blackburns were released. The judge was sympathetic to the escaped slaves, but the law was specific, leaving him no room for interpretation. The owners of the Blackburns won their case, and the judge ordered them returned to Kentucky on June 17.

The sentence of reenslavement created a great stir in Detroit, and on Sunday morning, June 16, a crowd mostly of black people, though a few white men were in attendance, was ready to storm the jail and

7. The Blackburns

free the prisoners. Some in the crowd were armed. In the midst of the threats that were not carried out that day, two black ladies — Mrs. Lightfoot and Mrs. French, who were members of the First Baptist Church — asked the sheriff for permission to visit Mrs. Blackburn to offer prayers and other support. Late in the afternoon two respectable, veiled ladies left the jail, crying, deeply anguished. The next morning Mrs. French was found sitting in the jail, and Ruthie had escaped across the river to Canada.

On the following day, Monday, June 17, the sheriff prepared to turn over Thornton to the representative of the Brown estate that still legally owned him. A group of armed and women marched to the jail, led by an old black woman who carried a white rag on top of a pole. When the sheriff saw the angry mob, he pulled Thornton back inside the jail. The chained Thornton was quick-witted, inventive, and convincing. He told the sheriff that if he could address the crowd, he would be able to get them homeward bound, peacefully, and then he would return to Kentucky.

Sheriff Wilson agreed, and Thornton appeared before the crowd. Immediately, someone tossed him a pistol. Members of the crowd called out urging him to shoot the jailer, who was on the steps with the sheriff. Instead, Thornton pointed the gun directly at Wilson, then shifted it, and shot heavenward. In the confusion that followed, the mob attacked the sheriff, seriously injuring him.

In a scene filled with local color, Thornton was dragged into a getaway cart by an old black woman called "Sleepy Polly," formerly a quiet woman, now a determined civil disobedient. The cart was driven by an old black man called "Daddy Walker," whose cart was pulled by a blind horse. By this time the mob of about 200 had grown to 400 or 500. Like abolitionists, underground conductors, many Quakers, and members of other religious groups, significant numbers of the mob believed that slavery was wrong and that a law mandating the return of runaway slaves should be disobeyed. The actions of the mob were considered a riot, and many black citizens of Detroit were arrested, including Mrs. French. Trials for 29 of those arrested began on June 21, and 11 were sent to jail, including "Daddy Walker."[18]

Thornton reached Canada West, and the Blackburns were now

free. They stayed in Sandwich, near Detroit, for a year. Ruthie abandoned her slave name and became "Lucie." The representative of the Brown estate made one last effort to reclaim Thornton; he crossed into Canada and requested the return of both Blackburns. He was in unfriendly territory. The proofs he had about the ownership of the two were denied, and even his credentials to represent the slave owners in Kentucky were considered invalid in Canada. The government officials completely denied his request,[19] just as members of the British government in Nassau protected Madison Washington and the slaves on the *Creole*. The British government had much to answer for in its part in allowing the extensive slave trade between Africa and the New World, but sympathetic officials began to act quickly to set free escaped slaves who arrived in British territories.

The Blackburns moved in 1834 to Toronto, where Thornton would have more opportunities. At first, he worked as a waiter at Osgoode Hall, home of the law courts. He saw the need for cab service and began a successful new career. The Blackburns bought a small shotgun house (three rooms in a row, without a hall) on land with room for a garden and orchard. He built a barn, with a hay loft, to shelter his horses. His business was successful, but the Blackburns lived modestly.[20]

The Blackburns lived in an area where many Ulster Protestants resided. An Anglican church was begun near their residence in 1843, and they subscribed to the building fund and became members of that congregation, another indication of their Canadian citizenship.[21]

From his earnings, Thornton was able to purchase several rental properties which then provided funds for him and his wife when he retired after the Civil War.

Once the Blackburns were in Toronto, they began helping escaped slaves. He had extensive contacts in the white and black communities and could give special help to male escapees. Lucie worked with Mrs. Willis and other members of the Anti-Slavery Society of Canada.[22] She was obviously useful in getting slave women settled, finding housing, and helping get children enrolled in school. The work of white and black women in the anti-slavery movement is still not fully known or appreciated. In the next chapter we show how the Blackburns helped the Jackson family.

7. The Blackburns

The Blackburns lived quiet lives, but they were also sociable. As members of the Anglican church, they were less intolerant of the drinking of alcohol than the more evangelical white and black churches. They served wine to their visitors, and Thornton had convivial friends. He twice appeared before a magistrate for drunken behavior. When he died in 1890, he left an estate of $18,000; five years later when Lucie died, her estate was valued at $13,000.[23]

In their lifetime, the Blackburns were not honored for their escape from slavery, jailing, rescue, and for their successful lives in Canada. He was an enterprising cab owner, and they both helped escaped slaves. Their story remained little known until Karolyn Smardz Frost published *I've Got a Home in Glory Land: A Lost Tale of the Underground Railroad* in 2007.

8

Ann Maria Jackson

Ann Maria Jackson and six of her children escaped from slavery in Delaware in November of 1858, helped initially by Quaker Thomas Garrett of Wilmington, Delaware, one of the most skilled Underground Railroad conductors.[1] Early in his life Garrett began assisting runaway slaves and was imaginative in his use of ruses to get them to freedom. In 1848, though, he was charged with aiding two slave children and was tried in federal court with Chief Justice Taney presiding. Garrett was found guilty and was heavily fined. He then addresses the court: "Judge, now that thee has relieved me of what little I possessed, I will go home and put another story on my house. I want room to accommodate more of God's poor."[2] Taney was not impressed with that remark and continued his pro-slavery rulings, culminating in the Dred Scott decision of 1857. In that decision, Taney wrote for the majority of the justices that black people could not sue in federal courts, for they had no rights: "They had for more than a century before been regarded as beings of an inferior order, ... they had no rights which the white man was bound to respect, and the negro might justly and lawfully be reduced to slavery for his benefit."[3]

After his conviction, Garrett continued his civil disobedience, helping escaped slaves and rejecting the findings of the Dred Scott decision. On September 21, 1858, he wrote William Still and James McKim of the Vigilance Committee in Philadelphia that he was sending along a woman and her six children, ages three or four to 16. All were soon to be sold and taken away, but they "preferred seeking their own master."[4]

Garrett reported that there were problems in getting the family out of Delaware safely because the younger children could not walk

8. Ann Maria Jackson

far, and it was not safe for the family to try to cross bridges, presumably because they were guarded. Garrett apparently sent a man in a carriage to pick the family up, but there were problems because of spies in the neighborhood. The driver returned the next day, but by this time the family was in another carriage, indicating that other abolitionists were helping them.[5] The Jacksons eventually arrived in Philadelphia and were interviewed and helped by the Vigilance Committee.

Still wrote in his book on the Underground Railroad that the mother of the children, Ann Maria Jackson, was of chestnut color and about 40 years old, good looking, and pleasant. "Her bearing," he noted, "was humble, as might have been expected, from the fact that she emerged from the lowest depths of Delaware Slavery."[6] Her master was a rich widower, a sly man, and a drinker, given to hard swearing. Some time before her escape, her master had taken two of her older children from her. She told Still that he "took my children away as soon as they were big enough to hand me a drink of water."[7]

Ann Maria's husband was free, and she had been able to live independently, hiring out as a laundress or white washer, and paying a yearly sum to her master. Her master gave her no expenses for the children, but when they were old enough to work, he could hire them out or sell them. For years she had to leave her house to go to work, not knowing what might happen to her unattended children. Her husband had no legal authority over his chil-

William Still helped large numbers of escaped slaves, interviewed them, and after slavery was abolished published his interviews in *The Underground Rail Road* (University of Illinois at Urbana-Champaign Library).

85

dren, for they were slaves. The loss of the older children preyed on his mind, and he died insane in the poor house shortly before his wife escaped.[8]

Ann Maria had earlier wanted to run away, but her husband had always objected. With his death, Still reported, she was determined to get "to some part of the world where she could have the control and comfort of her children."[9] On the road, the mother and her children were afraid that they would be betrayed, but they reached Philadelphia safely. There their stay was short, probably because of the danger from slave catchers, and they went on the Niagara City in Canada. There they were taken in by Hiram Wilson, who continued to help escapees. On November 30, 1858, Wilson wrote Still that he was sending the family on to Toronto where they would be better cared for. He provided letters of introduction to Thomas Henning and Mrs. Dr. Willis, both active in helping escapees.[10]

A volunteer social services network then came into play. Mrs. Willis and Mr. Henning of the Anti-Slavery Society of Canada took the large Jackson family to the Blackburn's small house.[11] The older boys perhaps slept in the hay loft of the barn on the property; the Jacksons were soon joined by James Henry, 17, Mrs. Jackson's son who escaped independently from Delaware. Just feeding the Jackson family would have been expensive for the Blackburns, but they were relatively well-off from his cab business and their investments in rental houses. The Jacksons could live with the Blackburns for a short time, but they needed housing, furniture, and jobs. Mrs. Willis, Mr. Henning, and the Blackburns had excellent contacts and could help Ann Maria find work as a laundress. They knew sympathetic people who could furnish Mrs. Jackson with washtubs and other necessary laundry equipment. They could find donated housing items and clothes for the destitute family. Mr. Blackburn, with his knowledge of people in Toronto gained from his years as a cab driver, could tell Mrs. Jackson and the older sons where jobs were. Mrs. Willis and Mr. Henning also had excellent contacts to help in finding jobs. Mrs. Blackburn undoubtedly helped find housing nearby and assisted in getting the younger children into school. The Blackburns were childless, and it seems they adopted the Jackson family.

8. Ann Maria Jackson

Mrs. Jackson began working as a laundress. James Henry went to work as a waiter at the fashionable Queen's Hotel.[12] Albert Jackson, after some time in school, became the first African-American–Canadian to be a member of the postal service in Toronto. At first, he was hidden from sight as a sorter of mail. The people of St. John's Ward, where the family lived, protested that he was not carrying the mail, and a committee of inquiry was established. Albert was soon allowed to carry mail.[13] These two Jackson children were doing well, but there was some prejudice against blacks in Toronto, as the keeping of Albert out of sight in the mail sorting room indicates.

Mrs. Jackson's son Richard (Dick) became a fashionable hairdresser, one who passed on the news and gossip of the day to many prominent citizens of Toronto as he shaved them and styled their hair. When he died in 1885, at the age of 38, a thousand people attended his funeral, including former mayors, aldermen, newspaper publishers, and many from the black community.[14] He was buried in the Blackburn family plot, indicating the closeness of the older family to the Jacksons.

Ann Maria was also buried in the Blackburn plot, which was next to the one purchased by George Brown, white editor of the Toronto *Globe* and a major supporter of the Anti-Slavery Society in Canada.[15] The two Jacksons and the Blackburns were buried alongside white citizens, an indication of advanced racial attitudes in this Canadian city.

The Jacksons in slavery had dismal prospects. William Still wrote in *The Underground Rail Road* that Mrs. Jackson was a brave and determined woman. He said of her just after she escaped: "The fire of freedom obviously burned with no ordinary fervor in the breast of this slave mother, or she never would have ventured with the burden of seven children, to escape from the hell of Slavery."[16] In Toronto she did the hard physical work of washing and ironing clothes until a year before her death. We know that her sons James Henry, Albert, and Richard all had good jobs. The history of the other children is lost, but it is reasonable to believe that they also became productive citizens in their new country.

9

Harriet Tubman

> Harriet Tubman had been their "Moses," ... She had faithfully gone down into Egypt, and had delivered these six bondmen by her own heroism. Harriet was a woman of no pretensions, indeed a more ordinary specimen of humanity could hardly be found among the most unfortunate-looking farm hands of the South. Yet, in point of courage, shrewdness and disinterested exertions to rescue her fellow-men, by making personal visits to Maryland among the slaves, she was without her equal.
> — William Still, *The Underground Rail Road*

Araminta Ross, who took the name Harriet Tubman, was born a slave to Harriet Green and Benjamin Ross in Maryland about 1820. She was a religious child, taught by her mother, and at the age of five, she was set to work taking care of a small white child. She was too young for such responsibilities, and she was often whipped and mistreated. At the age of seven, threatened with a beating for stealing a lump of sugar, she ran away and lived in a hog pen for five days. She was a sickly child, often returned to her mother to recuperate from illness or from bad treatment. She never learned to read and write. As she grew older, she was sent out to work in the fields where she developed into a strong field-hand.[1]

When she was about 15, during a confrontation between an overseer and a male slave, the overseer threw a heavy lead weight at the slave but hit Araminta in the head instead, fracturing her skull. She was ill for many weeks, and for the rest of her life she would sometimes fall into a deep sleep. She may have been suffering from narcolepsy, perhaps brought on by that injury. These states of deep sleep would come unexpectedly, even later in her life when she was leading slaves to freedom. She also had vivid dreams during these periods of sleep. One was of a mounted man kidnapping children. She could hear the sound of the horses' hooves and the cries of the slave mothers trying to save their children.[2]

She married John Tubman, a free black man, in 1844, and she began to think seriously of running away to a free state. In 1849, fearing she was soon to be sold, she left her husband and headed North. According to an interview with Tubman published in the *Freedmen's Record* in 1865, she said that on the evening before she escaped she was unable to tell anyone her plans for fear of being betrayed. Instead, she walked through the street singing "Good bye, I'm going to leave you, Good bye, I'll meet you in the kingdom."[3]

The reward notice for her in the local newspaper described her as "about 27 years" old, of chestnut color, "fine looking and bout 5 feet high."[4] There were anti-slavery supporters in the neighborhood, and she probably had help as she made her escape. Traveling by night and sleeping in a hidden spot during the day, she made her way to Philadelphia. Once she arrived there, she adopted her mother's name, Harriet, but retained her husband's family name. She found employment, probably doing domestic work, though it is not known exactly what jobs she undertook. She was always hard-working and self-sufficient and refused personal charity, but she did accept funds later when she was engaged in slave-stealing.[5]

A year after Harriet escaped, the Fugitive Slave Act mandated the return of escaped slaves to their masters. She was, then, in grave danger of being captured, but personal safety was not a concern for her. In the fall of 1850 she learned from a message sent by John Bowley, a free black man married to her niece Kaziah, that his wife and two children were to be sold at the end of the year. Harriet returned to Baltimore, and Bowley managed to get his wife and children to her. She kept her relatives in a safe place until she could get them to a free state. Bowley soon joined his family.[6]

Elated by her success, Tubman then returned to Maryland in the spring of 1851 and rescued one of her brothers and two other men. Six months later, in the autumn, she was again in Maryland wanting to convince her free husband to depart with her, but she found that he was now with another woman and had no intention of leaving Maryland. She dropped her husband out of her heart, but she did not marry again until after his death. Tubman went on with her rescue mission and in December brought out 11 people, including her brother William Henry and his fiancée. On this trip, she took the fugitives all the way to Canada, crossing at Niagara. "I wouldn't trust Uncle Sam with my people no longer," she said, "but I brought 'em clear off to Canada."[7]

For the next several years, Tubman made one or two trips a year, probably 19 in all, into the south to bring out those who wanted to be free. She was courageous, fierce, armed, and in control of those she was rescuing. She declared that if any man gave out, he would be shot.

"Would you really do that?" an interviewer for the 1865 *Freedmen's Record* asked her.

"Yes, if he was weak enough to give out, he'd be weak enough to betray us all, and all who had helped us; and do you think I'd let so many die just for one coward man."

"Did you ever have to shoot any one?"

"One time a man gave out the second night; his feet were sore and swollen, he couldn't go any further; he'd rather go back and die, if he must."

The other escapees argued with the man, bathed his feet, encouraged him, but he insisted on going back.

"I told the boys to get their guns ready, and shoot him. They'd have done it in a minute, but when he heard that, he jumped right up and went on as well as any body."[8]

She was amazingly resourceful. She gave laudanum to a baby to keep it from crying and alerting the patrols.[9] She trusted her instincts when posses were nearby and kept changing her plans to meet the dangers they faced on the escape routes. She worked alone when she was below the Mason-Dixon line, but once the fugitives were in a free state she had arrangements with William Still and other abolitionists and Underground Railroad conductors to get her charges on to Canada. She began to spend time in Canada each year. During the spring and summer months she most often worked as a domestic to earn money for her next trip down South.[10] In Canada, according to that interview published in the *Freedmen's Record* in 1865, she would collect clothing and "watch over the welfare" of those she had brought there. Her base

9. Harriet Tubman

of operation in Canada was in St. Catharines,[11] where the Rev. Hiram Wilson also resided and helped incoming slaves. She undoubtedly called on him for help in her activities. It wasn't just abolitionists she looked to for help. She believed she was in direct contact with God, who guided her in her work.[12]

When Benjamin Drew interviewed her for *The Refugee: A North-Side View of Slavery*, published in 1856, he seems to have known nothing of her activities as a slave-thief. Instead, she told him about her two sisters being sold away and about the feelings of hundreds of escaped slaves she had met: "I never saw one who was willing to go back and be a slave." But she agreed with many others interviewed by Drew that "We would rather stay in our native land, if we could be as free there as we are here."[13]

In 1857 she assisted her elderly parents to leave Maryland. They had been freed, and technically they could have departed without difficulty, but her father was under suspicion because of his own activities in helping escaping sleeves. Tubman realized that they should be quietly brought to Canada. She was sided by Thomas Garrett, and her parents were soon reunited with their five sons and other relatives living in Canada.[14]

In 1858 or 1859 Senator William Seward of Auburn, an anti-slavery supporter and an admirer of Tubman's activities, offered to sell her a large house in Auburn, New York, in the Finger Lakes region, on affordable terms.[15] She was then able to move her parents to a New York home, where, as they were free, they were not subject to the Fugitive Slave Act of 1850.[16] She continued to make dangerous trips into the south to bring out more slaves.

During the Civil war she worked as a nurse in army hospitals and with black refugees flowing behind Union lines. She also acted as a spy for the North. After the war, she established in Auburn a home for the old and poor. She never turned away anyone who appeared at her door for a meal or assistance. When she died in 1913, she was honored as the Moses of her people.[17] At an important time in Tubman's life, Canada was the promised land. Those she rescued from slavery were not safe in the United States after the passage of the Fugitive Slave Act in 1850, but they could live without fear in Canada.

10

John Fairfield, Southern Abolitionist Who Helped Slaves Escape to Canada[1]

"I would steal all the slaves in Virginia if I could," John Fairfield told the Quaker Levi Coffin, one of the most active conductors on the Underground Railroad. Fairfield was from a wealthy Virginia family of slaveholders who somehow turned against slavery. About 1849, when he was a young man, he decided to strike out for the free state of Ohio, leaving the cursed institution of involuntary servitude behind. He was determined to take his black friend Bill with him. Bill belonged to one of John's uncles, and the two had played together as boys and grown up together. Such childhood friendships were common enough in slave societies in the south, but it usually ended before the white boy reached adulthood. John never fit into the ways of the planter society, the friendship continued, and the two often talked about Bill escaping to Canada.[2]

The plan of escape was uncomplicated. On the night before John was to leave, Bill was to take one of his master's horses, meet John at a designated spot, and continue on to Ohio, Bill posing as John's servant. The two arrived safely in Ohio but determined it was not a safe spot and went on to Canada where Bill found work and was protected by the government of Queen Victoria.

Levi Coffin, known as president of the Underground Railroad, later asked Fairfield if he did not feel guilty for encouraging the theft of his uncle's horse and for slave stealing. John responded: "No! I knew that Bill had earned several horses for his master, and he took only one.

10. John Fairfield, Southern Abolitionist

Bill had been a faithful fellow, and worked hard for many years, and that horse was all the pay he got."[3] Fairfield certainly didn't feel guilty about his slave-stealing. Coffin consistently objected to such views, opposed as he was to horse-stealing or slave-stealing, though he would always give help to a runaway slave who reached a free state.

After a few months, John returned to Virginia, but his uncle suspected he had helped Bill escape and was making plans to have John arrested. To spite his uncle, John decided to take several slaves, including some belonging to his uncle, with him on his next trip to Canada. With John as guide, the group traveled by night and hid during the day. As they needed provisions, John would venture out during the day to make purchases. The group reached Canada safely, and John was reunited with Bill, now married.[4] Bill was obviously one of the most important people in John's life, but Coffin did not explore that subject in his memoirs, the source of most of our knowledge about John. Bill, we believe, enjoyed his life of freedom and did not join John later in slave-stealing ventures in the south. John decided to make his home in Canada, and he almost always returned there after each adventurous journey as slave-stealer.

Stories of John's slave-stealing circulated in the black refugee communities in Canada, and the escapees there began to ask him to rescue spouses, children, parents and friends still enslaved. Those who had money paid, but he would undertake the raid into enemy territory if no money changed hands. John was, Coffin declared, young and fond of excitement. John would question the Canadian refugees closely and learn where the captives were held, who their masters were, and any information that would help him take them out of bondage. He would then return south, adopt the pro-slavery attitudes of a Virginia planter, and even board in the big house of the prosperous slave-owner whose slaves he planned to free. He made his plans carefully with the slaves, who would quietly disappear, only to reappear in Canada.[5]

Fairfield helped several hundred slaves, but Coffin, a Quaker, had mixed feelings about John's activities. He admired John's courage but called him "a wicked man, daring and reckless in his actions, yet faithful to the trust reposed in him, and benevolent to the poor."[6] John was always heavily armed and never hesitated to use violence. Coffin opposed violence and urged John to stop his operations and settle down in Canada. John refused, and Levi went on helping refugees brought his way by John.

John used many ruses in finding the slaves he rescued. At times, he posed as a slave-trader as he made plans to round up slaves he intended to "steal." He would get them to the Underground Railroad, then return immediately to the south, adopting another disguise, using another scheme to free more blacks. He was sometimes arrested, but Coffin reports without explanation that John often managed to get out of jail because he was a Freemason, high in the Order.[7] Still, he suffered great deprivations in prison, and Coffin suggests he contracted tuberculosis. Poor health, though, never kept him away from his forays into the south. When he was especially ill, he stayed for a few weeks with the abolitionists John Rankin or Levi Coffin, but generally he stopped with black families when he was away from the south. He kept returning to Canada West where, it is reasonable to speculate, he was reunited with his childhood friend, Bill, and with other slaves he had rescued.

Some of John's most daring exploits were in arranging for the escape of light-skinned mulattoes and quadroons. Their relatives in Canada raised the necessary money, and John proceeded to Philadelphia, where he bought powder and wigs for $80. He met the would-be fugitives in Washington, D.C., Virginia, and Maryland, powdered the profusely, put the wigs on them, bought train tickets for them, and smuggled them out as white people. Once that group was safe in Canada, he returned to Washington, D.C., and with powder and wigs outfitted another group of slaves. They, too, reached Canada without incident. There were others to be helped the same way, but when he returned to Philadelphia to buy more supplies, he did not have enough money to pay for these disguises. He then applied for help at an abolitionist society and gave Coffin as a reference.

The society wired Coffin: "John Fairfield wants money; shall we give it to him?"

Coffin responded, "If John Fairfield needs money, give it to him."[8]

Once again with funds, John traveled into Virginia, near Harpers Ferry, where more slaves were powdered and wigged. One had to be

10. John Fairfield, Southern Abolitionist

left behind, though, for his skin was too dark to be disguised by powder. The rest of the escapees were put on the express train to Pittsburgh. The slaves were soon missed, and in a scene similar to those often played out in western movies, the slave-catchers engaged an engine and one car, and the posse set out at high speed to overtake the express train before it reached Pittsburgh, doing so just as the express came into the station. The wheels of the express train still turning slowly, the powdered and wigged blacks sprang out and scattered in every direction, the posse in pursuit. No one was captured. Within a few days, the blacks reached Canads.[9]

A refugee slave once told Coffin that Fairfield told those wanting to escape that he would rescue them "or die in the attempt, if we would do our part, which we promised to do. We all agreed to fight till we died, rather than be captured. Fairfield said he wanted no cowards in the company; if we were attacked and one of us showed cowardice or started to run, he would shoot him down."[10]

Coffin, devoted to peace principles, reproved John for such views: "I told him it was better to suffer wrong than to do wrong, and that we should love our enemies."[11]

"Love the devil!" he responded. "Slaveholders are all devils, and it is no harm to kill the devil. I do not intend to hurt people if they keep out of the way, but if they step in between me and liberty, they must take the consequences. When I undertake to conduct slaves out of bondage I feel that it is my duty to defend them, even to the last drop of my blood."[12]

Coffin saw that it did no good to preach Quaker principles to Fairfield, but his conscience was elastic, and he went on helping John and the escaping slaves.

What happened to the daring Fairfield? Coffin did not have explicit information, but he thought it possible his friend was in Tennessee in 1861 as the war was beginning. Slaves along the Cumberland River acquired arms and rose up in revolt, instigated by a white man. Armed whites then hunted down the insurrectionists, including a white man who was killed and whose name was not known. Coffin concluded, "I have always supposed that this man was John Fairfield, and that in this way his strange career was ended by a violent death. With all his faults and misguided impulses, and wicked ways, he was a brave man; he never betrayed a trust that was reposed in him, and he was a true friend to the oppressed and suffering slave."[13]

Few stories about the Underground Railroad have more conflicts than the story of Bill, John, and Levi: a young white Virginian who turned against the pro-slavery views of his class and became a notorious slave-stealer; the life-long friendship of a white Virginian born into the planter class with a slave who had been his childhood playmate; a non-violent Quaker who befriended a slave-stealer who used violent means. Coffin deplored that violence, castigated John's methods and yet admired the accomplishments of the Virginian attempting to free every slave he possibly could and get them safely to Canada.

11

Chaplain Garland H. White

> The historian pen cannot fail to locate us somewhere among the good and the great, who have fought and bled upon the alter of their country.
>
> — Garland H. White[1]

Garland H. White was born a slave about 1829 in Hanover County, Virginia.[2] When he was a child, he was sold to Robert Toombs, a Georgia politician who served in Washington in the House of Representatives from 1845 to 1853 and in the Senate from 1853 until 1861. Toombs was a wealthy, mercurial man, not even tempered and overly fond of strong drink. He favored the Fugitive Slave Act of 1850, and during his many years in Congress he consistently supported southern causes. White was Toombs's body servant, living with him in both Georgia and Washington, D.C., and Toombs could hardly have been an easy master.[3] As early as 1850 there was unrest among Toombs's household slaves in Washington; one of them escaped and was wounded in an ambush before he could get outside the confines of the District of Columbia. He managed to get away nevertheless. From this hazardous escape of a fellow slave, White had dramatic evidence of the dangers of fleeing.[4] Little is known of White's early years and his treatment in slavery, but he somehow learned to read and write, and, like Frederick Douglass, was a quick learner.

In September of 1859, in Georgia, White was licensed to preach the gospel, probably as a minister of the African Methodist Episcopal (AME) Church, though the name of the church is not given in the surviving documents.[5]

After Toombs and White returned to the nation's capitol that year, White fled to Canada. What difficulties he encountered and just where he first settled are not known. Perhaps he had some additional months of education, for he was a fluid writer, well-organized and with a large vocabulary, though his spelling was not always standard.

In October 1861 White was appointed by Bishop Green to be in charge of the London, Canada West, AME Mission.[6] Four or five years earlier, when Benjamin Drew was at work on *The Refugee: A North-Side View of Slavery*, London had a population of 12,000, about 350 of whom were black. White's church work would have been carried out with difficulty, for as Drew noted, whites were prejudiced against blacks in London. Schools were open to all, but black children were discriminated against and few attended.[7] The racial situation in London had probably not improved by 1861. White was, however, living free, a new experience for him.

In early May of 1862, the Rev. White wrote to Edwin M. Stanton, Union secretary of war, that blacks were willing "to serve as soldiers in the southern parts during the summer season or longer if required." It was then believed that blacks were more immune than whites to yellow fever and malaria, then prevalent during summer months. White offered to recruit troops and leave Canada which was "free from all the calumnities of your land" in order to serve "his suffering countrymen."[8] President Lincoln had been refusing to allow blacks to enlist in the Union armed forces, and Stanton did not bother to respond to White's letter. After the Emancipation Proclamation became effective on January 1, 1863, black troops were authorized to join the Union armed services.

Perhaps in anticipation of playing a role in recruiting troops, the Rev. White left Canada and by January 1863 was ministering to a church in Toledo, Ohio. White's wife and daughter joined him there.[9]

Recruiting was not easy for White or Mary Ann Shadd Cary, or others, even though blacks tended to believe that a Union victory would mean the end of slavery. For many months, black enlistees were paid much less than whites, and stories about racial prejudice in the Union armed forces were certainly known in the black community. Also, blacks had to serve in segregated units in the Union army, with a white

11. Chaplain Garland H. White

officer in command. White wrote: "I have recruited colored men for every colored regiment raised in the north, forsaken my church & canvassed the intire north and west urging my people to inlist & have succeeded in every instant."[10] He received $15 for every recruit. His goal was to be appointed a chaplain.

Late in 1863 he was working particularly in Indiana, and he claimed to have recruited half of the 28th United States Colored Infantry regiment in that state. According to army regulations, a chaplain could not be appointed until the regiment was at full strength, and it was not. The Rev. White then joined the Indiana 28th Colored Infantry as a private on January 4, 1864. He continued his work as a recruiter and began to act, unofficially, as chaplain, serving under Lt. Col. Charles E. Russell, the white officer sympathetic to blacks who requested his assignment. The Indiana 28th departed on April 24, 1864, for Washington and joined the Army of the Potomac. White was obviously a true believer in the Union cause, for he wrote Secretary of State Seward that he had enlisted "to be with my boys & should I fail to get my commission I shall willingly serve my time out."[11] He asked for help in securing a commission as chaplain.

Secretary Seward then did recommend White, noting that he had known him "when he was a slave of Robert Toombs and I knew him afterwards in Canada." Seward was a long-time foe of slavery, and perhaps played some role in White's escape from Toombs. Lt. Col. Russell was asked about White and responded: "It is the wish of most of the officers that ... White should receive the appointment of Chaplain his having been very useful as acting officer for the regy."[12] The appointment was still not made.

Although White continued to recruit and to act as chaplain, he was obviously restless. He wrote Secretary Seward on July 19, 1864, suggesting that he be added to General Sherman's army, then in Georgia, "to act as a guide." He pointed out that he was acquainted with the large plantations along the Chattahoochee River and with Toombs's plantation in Stewart County on the river about 36 miles below Columbus. He noted that he had traveled the entire area by railroad, steam boat, and by country roads. He made a compelling argument: "If it is the policy of the government to take the slaves from the Enemy & use them in putting down the Rebellion why not send me to a part ... where I know the people & the Roads and country generally."[13] White did not get this assignment, but his willingness to lead Union forces to Toombs's plantation and others in that fertile area shows exactly how he felt about Toombs and his desire to end slavery.

Although he was not sent to Georgia as a guide, White remained in the Indiana 28th in Virginia and observed the "Battle of the Crater" on July 30, 1864. In the trench warfare around Petersburg, Virginia, the Union and Confederate forces were often only 100 yards apart, with firing going on day and night. As a way of breaking the impasse, white coal miners in the 48th Pennsylvania dug a tunnel under the Confederate gun position and packed it with four tons of powder. Originally, several regiments of well-trained black troops were to charge the rebel lines immediately after the explosion, take Petersburg, and thus make Richmond, long a target of Union forces, vulnerable. At the last moment, General Grant decided to send in unprepared white soldiers leading the charge. Grant later said that he did not want the public to think he was using black troops as cannon fodder.

At 4:45 in the morning on July 30, the powder was ignited, creating a crater 170 feet long, 60 feet wide, and 30 feet deep, causing massive death and destruction to the Confederate forces.[14] The Rev. White described the scene in a letter to the *Christian Recorder*, an AME magazine, written on August 20, 1864: "...the earth began to shake, as though the hand of God intended a reversal of the laws of nature. This grand convulsion sent both soil and souls to inhabit the air for a while, and then returned to be commingled forever with each other, as the word of God commands, 'From dust thou art, and unto dust thou shalt return.'"[15] The unprepared Union troops rushed into the crater itself instead of going around it, and the rebels began a fierce counterattack. Black troops were called in then. According to White, the colored troops, led by white Colonel Charles E. Russell performed well, but Petersburg was not taken. The casualty figures vary but about 4,000 Union troops, black and white, were killed or wounded in the Battle of the Crater. Col. Russell reported that the Indiana 28th lost about 100 killed, wounded, or missing.[16] The Rev. White was a realist; he understood that the Union generals blundered in not utilizing their best

11. Chaplain Garland H. White

trained white and black troops in the early stages of the battle. White argues convincingly that the black troops were not cowards, as some in the North were charging.

Just as Col. Russell was ordering, "Fix bayonets; charge bayonets!" he said to the chaplain, "Brother White, good-bye, Take care of yourself—for today someone must die, and if it be me, I hope our people will get the benefit of it."[17] Col. Russell used "brother" in several senses: a reference to a male member of the same church, a reference to a fellow human being, and as an indication of military bonding. Given the context, Russell probably meant all of these. The two men were undoubtedly both Protestants, and Russell may well have been a Methodist, as was White. The colonel also clearly admired White's work as an unofficial chaplain and regarded him as an admirable human being, a brother. Col. Russell may also have had in mind Shakespeare's King Henry V who gave a rousing speech to the troops before the battle of Agincourt:

> From this day to the ending of the world,
> But we in it shall be remembered—
> We few, we happy few, we band of brothers;
> For he to-day that sheds his blood with me
> Shall be my brother; be he ne'er so vile,
> This day shall gentle his condition;
> And gentlemen in England, now a-bed,
> Shall think themselves accurs'd they were not here;
> And hold their manhoods cheap whiles any speaks
> That fought with is upon Saint Crispin's day (IV.iii.58–67).

Col. Russell survived and remained White's brother.

White was committed to his fellow troops in the Union army and to the war effort, and he did not complain about the inequities in pay suffered by black troops. He wrote the *Christian Recorder* on September 8, 1864, published on September 17, that a "few colored regiments from Massachusetts make much fuss, and complain more than all the rest of the colored troops of the nation. They are doing themselves and their race a serious injury. I sincerely hope they will stop such nonsense, and learn to take things as soldiers should. It is not that they are undergoing any more than we are."[18]

The War Department finally approved White as regimental chaplain, and on October 25, 1864, he was discharged as a private and commissioned, receiving the pay of a captain — $100 a month and rations. There were only 14 black chaplains in the Union army.[19]

Chaplain White did not write the *Christian Recorder* the next few months, and his activities during the winter of 1864–1865 are not known. After General Robert E. Lee abandoned Richmond, Virginia, on April 2, 1865, White had a momentous day. Union companies rushed to be the first to enter the long-besieged Confederate capital, and White marched at the head of his regiment, which was one of the first to enter that city. The officers and men of his regiment asked him to give a speech to the 10,000 people gathered on Broad Street. The slave pens had been opened, and thousands had come out "praising God" and "Father, or Master Abe." That day, White remarked, for the first time in Richmond "freedom to all mankind" was proclaimed. White was in such a state of excitement, he forgot parts of his speech.

White's regiment marched on to Camp Lee, and in the crowd there an old woman was looking for her son Garland, taken from her as a child to serve Robert Toombs. During the war, she had talked with Toombs, who was secretary of state for the Confederacy and then general of the Georgia forces serving in Virginia. Toombs told her that Garland had run away to Canada but was then living in Ohio.[20] It is not known how Toombs knew White's whereabouts, but it is possible that White, like many another escaped slave, wrote to his former master describing his life in freedom and his accomplishments as a free man.

One of the men in White's regiment came to him, saying, "Chaplain, here is a lady that wishes to see you." He followed the soldier to a group of black women, where he was asked questions:

> "What is your name, sir?"
> "What was your mother's name?"
> "Where were you born?"

He answered then questions in all and was then told, "This is your mother ... who has spent twenty years of grief about her son."[21] He had not recognized her. Other writers in 1865 might well have continued the story with a sentimental scene, but White wisely leaves the emo-

11. Chaplain Garland H. White

tions of that meeting to the imagination of the reader. Similar scenes were being carried out that day in Richmond, and in the following months they continued to be played out.

Later that day, April 4, 1865, the Union army staged a grand parade for President Lincoln and General Grant. It was a time of exuberance and pride for White and for the United States colored troops. White was ready to stay with his regiment until freedom was "proclaimed throughout the world."[22]

A few days later, White was called upon to carry out one of the most difficult duties assigned to a chaplain. At 10 P.M. on April 19, 1865, the orderly of Brevet General Russell came to White's tent, woke him, and gave him this written order:

> Rev. Garland H. White, Chaplain of the 28th Colored Troops:
>
> Sir:—You are requested to call upon Samuel Mapps,* private in Co. D., 10th U.S.C.T., now under sentence of death, and now confined in the Bull-pen,† to prepare him to meet his Savior.
> By official orders
> Gen. C.S. Russell§
> T. Latchford, Assist, Adj. Gen.

Chaplain White responded:

> Gen. C.S. Russell, Commanding this Post:
>
> Sir:—I have the honor to acknowledge receipt of your order respecting my visiting private Samuel Mapps, Co. D, 10th U.S.C.T. In reply, I would say I will comply promptly, and do all in my power to point him to the Lamb of God that taketh away the sins of the world.[23]

The two letters follow protocol, and the general's order is race neutral and indicates that White is regarded highly by his senior officer. White's response shows that he would follow the command, even though he may have had qualms since the condemned Mapp was black. To the modern reader, the ease with which religion is mentioned in these official letters is somewhat startling.

---

*Mapp is the correct spelling.
†A barred enclosure in a jail.
§For his service in the Battle of the Crater, Russell had been promoted. The S in his name is apparently correct. His name in some places is given as Charles E. Russell.

At the prison, White began his meeting with Mapp: "Well, my friend, how stands your case?"

Pvt. Mapp pled his innocence and began to rehearse the events of his trial. White responded: "I came to see you, not to discuss a point of law as to the nature of your trial and decision, for that is all useless, and, my friend, I must tell you that to-day, at 12 o'clock you will be executed — yes, you will be shot. Now, let you and myself kneel down and address a throne of grace where you may obtain mercy and help in time of need."

White describes in detail the prayers that were said. Then a wagon, with guards, arrived at the bull-pen. The Rev. White told Mapp to stand up and walk with him to the wagon, where both sat on Mapp's coffin. They were taken to an open field, about a mile away, where a large crowd had gathered.

Again, the Rev. White reported his prayers as Mapp faced the firing squad. His last words to the prisoner were, "Good-by, my brother, good-by."[24] In the highly-charged emotions of war, Col. Russell, Chaplain White, and Pvt. Mapp were all a band of brothers. The order to fire was given, and soon White approached the lifeless body of Mapp, five or six bullets in the heart. "It was the saddest spectacle I ever witnessed, and I hope never to witness another the longest day I live."[25]

The chaplain concluded by saying that Mapp had attempted to kill his captain, and that he was also found guilty of insubordination. Mapp "was a Virginian," he wrote, "and had never lived North."[26] "North" includes Canada, and White implies that had Mapp escaped slavery and lived as a free man, he would have understood freedom and would not have defied the authority of the officer who was a leader in a war that would free slaves. White does not seem to have been aware that Mapp had been protesting the inequities of pay in the Union army. White had earlier objected to such protests.

After the war was over, White was sent with the 28th United States Colored Infantry to Corpus Christi, Texas. In his letter of September 19, 1865, to the *Christian Recorder* he argued that the black codes being passed in the South tended to return the newly-freed slaves to a state of semi-slavery. President Andrew Johnson was awarding amnesty to former Confederates, allowing them to vote, and at the same time the Black Codes were restricting the rights of blacks. The Rev. White then wrote words that easily could have been spoken by Dr. Martin Luther King, Jr., a century later: "I am glad to see that there are some, both white and colored, who think as we think, and are determined to do all they can to arouse the mind of the nation to a sense of its duty. May they continue to speak until the bonds of ignorance are riven — till dark oppression is driven from the earth — till from every land and every sea, one universal, triumphant song is heard, to hail every slave at liberty."[27]

Conditions for soldiers and for the citizens around Corpus Christi were terrible. Food was scarce and malaria and other diseases common. The mortality rate for troops was high, and White wrote, "Going to the grave with the dead is as common to me as going to bed."[28] He presided at funeral services for the dead of other regiments, too, for chaplains were scarce. He had met only one other in Texas. The countryside was desolate, and he had not seen enough foodstuffs "to fatten a six months' pig."[29] He was not certain how the former rebels were going to live through the winter, and it is clear that he had considerable sympathy for them. White was a humane man, defending black troops called cowards, helping a condemned man face the firing squad, wanting to spread freedom to the entire world, and showing concern about the conditions of former rebels in Texas.

White was conscientious in his religious duties in Texas. He conducted services on Sunday and prayer services two nights each week. He did report that "profane swearing is too prevalent with both officers & with men," and he noted that only two officers were religious. He wanted to open a school but had no supplies, but he had 300 troops who could "Read Write & Cipher" and 474 who could spell and read.[30]

The Rev. White was discharged on January 9, 1866, and returned to Toledo and his church there. He had begun having lung problems during his army service — perhaps he suffered from tuberculosis — and seems to have been ill much of the rest of his life. In 1872 he moved to Halifax, North Carolina. He received a small pension of $6 a month and eventually he was unable to continue as a clergyman. The pension was then raised to $14. He moved to Washington, D.C., and made repeated appeals for an increase in his pension, but these requests were denied. He died in Washington, probably in 1894, but his pension file does not contain the month or year.[31]

The Rev. White was a worthy man, dedicated to freedom and obviously influenced by his years in Canada, where he lived as a free man. His experiences there obviously had great influence upon him, though it must be admitted that his life in London, Canada West is unknown. It is only in recent times that he had been recognized for his service to his country of birth.

12

Dr. A.T. Augusta

Alexander Thomas Augusta was born a free black in 1825 in Norfolk, Virginia. When he was a child, he was taught to read, and he increased his reading skills when he was an apprentice to a barber. Wishing to study medicine, he moved to Baltimore where he received private tutoring. He relocated to Philadelphia and applied for admission to the University of Pennsylvania medical school but was denied. A sympathetic professor of medicine allowed Augusta to study in his office. Augusta applied to a medical school in Chicago but again was rejected. Trinity Medical College in Toronto accepted him, and he and his wife, Mary O. Burgoin, moved to Canada.[1]

Both Augustas had to work hard to meet their expenses during his student days. She opened a "New Fancy Dry Goods and Dressmaking Establishment."[2] He owned a drugstore that filled prescriptions, sold over-the-counter medicines, and offered several other services: "Leeches applied. Cupping, Bleeding, and Teeth Extracted."[3] He graduated in 1856 and during the next few years was in private practice, in charge of the city hospital, and was physician for the local poor house. He was mentor to Anderson Ruffin Abbot, another black man, during Dr. Abbott's medical training, and the men became close friends.[4]

After the Civil War began, Dr. Augusta traveled to Washington, D.C., to take the medical examination necessary for appointment to the Union medical corps. Just days after the Union began accepting Black enlistees, on January 7, 1863, Dr. Augusta wrote President Lincoln and Secretary of War Stanton about his desire to serve as a physician and surgeon in the Union armed forces. He was rejected two months later because he was of African descent and because he was "an alien and a British subject." He responded that he expected to serve a black regiment and that although his medical degree was from a Canadian college, he had not given up his United States citizenship.[5]

Dr. Augusta's explanation was accepted, and he underwent an oral examination to test his medial skills. The examiner was Dr. Cronyn. Dr. Augusta passed, and later Surgeon General Hammond asked, "I say Cronyn how did you come to let that nigger pass?" Dr. Cronyn replied, "The fact is, general, that the nigger knew more than I did and I could not help myself."[6]

The Union Army Medical Board on April 1, 1863, found Dr. Augusta "Qualified for the position of surgeon of the Negro regiment now being raised." Only eight black men served as physicians in the Union army. He was appointed to the Seventh U.S. Colored Infantry, the first black to serve as a doctor in the U.S. army.[7]

Dr. Augusta was subjected to racial taunts and attacks. In uniform, he was on his way from Baltimore to Philadelphia. When he arrived at the Baltimore train station, two men, angered to see a black officer, attacked him and tore off his insignia. A mob then gathered and threatened his life. Guards arrived and escorted him to the office of the provost marshal, where Dr. Augusta produced his commission papers. The army then acted quickly on his behalf. The Lt. Colonel in the office provided Dr. Augusta with an armed guard. On the way back to the station, Dr. Augusta recognized two of his attackers, and they were immediately arrested. As they proceeded, a man suddenly appeared and punched Dr. Augusta in the nose, causing blood to flow freely. The guards arrested that man, and with guns drawn, delivered Dr. Augusta to the station. There an officer on the staff of General Joseph Hooker agreed to accompany the doctor on the train trip, for it was feared he was still in danger. Dr. Augusta later reported that he had "always known Baltimore as a place where it is considered a virtue to mob colored people."[8] He had left the safety of life in Canada "to bind up the wounds of those colored men who should volunteer, as well as those rebels and copperheads whom the fortune of war might throw into my hands."[9] He saw himself treating blacks, captured Confederates, and Northern sympathizers to the Southern cause, but he does not mention white Union soldiers. The army had removed him as medical officer for that group.

12. Dr. A.T. Augusta

Dr. Augusta, highly qualified in medicine, was soon named the officer in charge of Freemen's Hospital, the first black to be in charge of a United States hospital. He continued to be faces with racism, and in February 1864 several white physicians objected to serving under him, and he was reassigned to a recruiting office in Baltimore. His army unit was sent to Beaufort, South Carolina, and he spent the rest of the war there.[10]

Dr. Augusta was subjected to many indignities while he served in the army. Although he was promoted to Major, he was paid as if he were an enlisted man. Senator Henry Wilson of Massachusetts had to intervene to get him paid properly. He did assert his rights when he was discriminated against. On February 1, 1864, he was in Washington, D.C., on his way to testify at a court-martial and was ordered to sit in the "Negro" section of the street car. He refused and was removed from the car. He arrived late for the hearing and explained the circumstances to the judge advocate. This matter of discrimination reached the Senate, and as a result the street cars were desegregated, at least for a time.[11]

In March 1865 Dr. Augusta was serving as Brevet Lt. Colonel, the first black to achieve that rank, and the highest rank achieved by a black man in the Union army. After the war, he joined the medical faculty of Howard University in 1868, the first black to receive an appointment in a United States medical school. His achievements meant nothing in the white medical world. In 1869 he applied for admission to the Medical Society of the District of Columbia and was rejected because of his race. He later helped establish, in 1884, the Medical-Chirurgical Society of D.C., the first black medical society in the country. He died in 1890.[12]

Dr. Augusta's medical education in Canada allowed him to succeed in Canada and in the United States, but in the country of his birth he was often subjected to humiliating racial discrimination. He and his friend Dr. Abbott, however, were properly greeted by Lincoln in the White House. For an account of these black doctors at the White House, see the following chapter on Dr. Abbot.

13

The Abbott Family

Wilson Ruffin Abbott

Wilson Ruffin Abbott was born a free black in Richmond, Virginia, in 1801, to a father who was Scotch-Irish and a mother who was a free black. Apprenticed at an early age to a carpenter, Wilson ran away, worked for a time at a hotel in Alabama, then was a steward on a Mississippi riverboat. Injured when a stack of wood fell on him, he was nursed back to health by a maid, Ellen Toyer. She taught him to read and write, and he had a natural talent for mathematics. Wilson and Ellen were married and established a successful grocery in Mobile, Alabama, but they were soon subjected to severe discriminatory laws. The city council passed an ordinance requiring all free blacks to post a bond signed by two white men and to wear badges indicating they were bonded. Abbott refused, and shortly thereafter he received an anonymous letter indicating that his store was going to be destroyed and warning him to leave Mobile immediately. He took the letter seriously, removed all his money from the bank, and put his wife and children on a boat for New Orleans. He departed the next day, and his store was soon looted, a total loss. The white merchants had protected their businesses from competition.[1]

The Abbotts lived for a time in New York, but because of discrimination there left for Toronto in 1835. Abbott was a skilled businessman and became a real-estate broker and a major property owner, his holdings including 42 houses and a warehouse.[2]

Concerned about the education of his nine children, in 1850 he moved his family to Elgin, near Chatham, for a time in order for them to attend the highly-regarded Buxton Mission School.

13. The Abbott Family

Wilson Abbott considered himself Canadian and never returned to the United States. He and his wife, Ellen Toyer Abbott, were active in church and civic activities in Toronto. She founded the Queen Victoria Benevolent Society to aid refugees coming into Toronto. Known as a substantial citizen, Wilson Abbott was elected to the Toronto City Council. He died in 1876, a respected Canadian.[3]

Dr. Anderson Ruffin Abbott

Wilson's son Anderson Ruffin Abbott[4] was born in Toronto in 1837. He attended Canadian schools and then enrolled in Oberlin College in Ohio for three years before studying medicine at the University of Toronto. Dr. A.T. Augusta was his mentor during his medical school days, and the two men became close friends. Abbott was the first Canadian-born black physician. He received his medical degree and was licensed to practice in 1861.[5] Committed to the cause of black freedom, Dr. Abbott requested that Secretary of War Stanton give him a medical appointment in the Union army, and in 1863 he was commissioned as an assistant surgeon, one of eight black men to serve as doctors in the Union army. Dr. Abbott served as a physician at a camp for slaves who had escaped from the Confederacy. This camp was directed by Dr. Augusta. The two young doctors were involved in the founding of the Freedmen's Hospital in Washington, D.C.[6]

During the winter of 1863–1864, Drs. Abbott and Augusta, in dress uniforms, attended a levee in the East Room of the White House and met President Lincoln. As the two men entered the receiving room, President Lincoln came forward and took Dr. Augusta's hand. Robert Todd Lincoln, son of President and Mrs. Lincoln, was standing about six paces away, with his mother, and came to his father, asking a question hastily: "Are you going to allow this innovation?"

"Why not?" Mr. Lincoln responded, and Robert returned to his mother's side. Mr. Lincoln shook the doctor's hand, and then Dr. Abbott was introduced and his hand was shaken also. Mrs. Lincoln was less concerned than her son about the presence of medical men of color in the White House. After the assassination of the president, she gave Dr. Abbott a plaid shawl her husband had often worn.[7]

The two physicians then entered the East Room, Dr. Abbott wrote, "which was crowded and brilliantly lit up." They "became the cynosure of all eyes.... I suppose it was a first time in the history of the U.S. when a colored man had appeared at one of these levees. What made us more conspicuous of course was our uniforms. Colored men in the uniforms of U.S. military officers of high rank had never been seen before."[8]

At the end of the Civil War, Dr. Abbott returned to Canada and enrolled for additional medical courses at the University of Toronto. In 1869 he was admitted to the province's College of Physicians and Surgeons. He practiced in Toronto and other towns and cities in Canada, while always taking part in civic affairs and speaking against segregated schools and in favor of classical education for black children.

In 1891, Dr. Abbott retired and moved to Chicago. He was soon asked to take a position at the recently-founded Provident Hospital and Training School Association.[9] Emma Reynolds, a young black woman, applied to the various nursing schools in Chicago and was rejected by all of them because of her race. Her brother approached a well-known black surgeon, Dr. Daniel Hale Williams, about opening a hospital and nursing school for blacks. Funds were raised to make a down payment on a three story house at 29th and Dearborn. The 12-bed hospital opened in 1891 with Dr. Williams as chief-of-staff. Dr. Williams left for Washington, D.C., in 1894, and Dr. Abbott came out of retirement to become medical superintendent at the hospital, a position he held for three years.[10]

Like his father, Dr. Abbott was a shrewd investor, and after he left Provident Hospital he was largely concerned with managing his financial affairs. About 1900 he returned to Toronto. As his father had been, he was accepted in Toronto society and did not suffer racial discrimination there. He was a man of many interests, and he wrote on medicine, race, Darwinism, and the need for integrated schools. He died in 1913, a Canadian citizen of distinction.[11]

14

John Henry Hill

> John Henry never forgot those with whom he had been a fellow-sufferer in Slavery; he was always fully awake to their wrongs, and longed to be doing something to aid and encourage such as were striving to get their Freedom. He wrote many letters in behalf of others, as well as for himself, the tone of which, was always marked by the most zealous devotion to the slave, a high sense of the value of Freedom, and unshakable confidence that God was on the side of the oppressed, and a strong hope, that the day was not far distant, when the slave power would be "suddenly broken and that without remedy."
> —William Still, *The Underground Rail Road*

In September 1853, John Henry Hill escaped from Virginia to Philadelphia and was interviewed by William Still, who later wrote about the fugitive in *The Underground Rail Road*: Hill was six feet tall, brown in color, "with marked intellectual features."[1] A carpenter, he was married to a free black woman and had children. During the year of 1852, Hill had hired himself out, paying his owner $150. On January 1, 1853, John Mitchell, his owner, took Hill from Petersburg to Richmond. Hill was unaware of Mitchell's plan until they were going into a building, and someone produced handcuffs to secure Hill. He then realized that he was entering an auction house where he would be sold. He turned on his would-be captors, and fought them with "fist, knife, and feet, so tiger-like," Still wrote, "that he actually put four or five men to flight, his master among the number."[2] He was able to run away that day, but it took him months to get out of Virginia.[3] He wrote out for Still an account of that period of his life. He had learned to read and write, and his written statement shows that he wrote clearly and was well-organized, though his spelling and punctuation are not always standard: "I was secreted for a long time in a kitchen of a merchant, at Richmond, where I was taken care of by a lady friend of my mother. When I got Tired of staying in that place, I wrote myself a pass to pass myself to Petersburg, here I stopped with a very prominent Colored person, who was a friend to Freedom stayed there until two white friends told other friends if I was in the city to tell me to go at once ... because they had hard [heard] a plot."[4]

Hill then wrote himself another pass and returned to the same den in Richmond where he had earlier spent a month. On September 12, 1853, he was able to secure a private berth on the steamer *City of Richmond* for $125, undoubtedly including a bribe to the captain. He was determined not to be returned to slavery: "I had started from my Den that morning for Liberty or Death providing myself with a Brace of Pistels."[5]

John Henry Hill was helped by William Still and corresponded with Still after reaching Canada (University of Illinois at Urbana-Champaign Library).

Hill landed in Philadelphia and was taken in by the Vigilance Committee and interviewed by Still. Hill was concerned about his wife and two children, but they were free, and he knew they could be brought away from Virginia. After a few days, he went on to Toronto, and by October 4, 1853, he wrote Still that he had immediately found work, probably as a carpenter.

Hill wrote Still again on October 30, 1853. Still had sent Hill's trunk on to Toronto, and when Hill went to the Custom House to pay the duty, the agent asked, "Are these your effects?"

"Yes."

"Are you going to settle in Canada?"

"Yes."

The agent then asked Hill to tell his story. After Hill finished, the

14. John Henry Hill

agent said, "I am happy to see you and all that will come."⁶ While citizens of Canada were often hostile to blacks, almost all government officials welcomed them and, when necessary, acted to protect their rights.

Hill concluded that Canada was a hospitable country, and he thought runaway slaves should come to that northern land. In his next letter to Still, undated, but probably in November 1853, he expanded on his earlier impressions: "So I ask you to send the fugitives to Canada. I don't know much of this Province but I beleaves that there is Rome [room] enough for the colored and whites of the United States. We want farmers mechanic men of all qualification &c, if they are not made [trained] we will make them, if we cannot make the old, we will make our children."⁷ He showed his training as a builder when he praised the beauty of Toronto but lamented that too many of the "codages" were made of wood; he wrote "I am in hopes there will be more of the Brick and Stonn."⁸

In that same letter, Hill lamented that his owners in Virginia denied him an education, otherwise he would have confronted slaveholders with words of truth making them tremble with he spoke, and their knees would smote together."* He went on to praise the British laws which protected him from bloodhounds, but he argued that blacks in Canada should depend upon themselves and strengthen themselves. In this respect, he was filled with Emersonian optimism and the belief in self-reliance common in North American thinking at that time. Ideas from Emerson's essay on "Self-Reliance" (1841) were in the air, though it is not likely Hill actually read Emerson's essay. He would have agreed, though, with this Emersonian sentence which ended "Self Reliance":

"Nothing can bring you peace but yourself. Nothing can bring you peace but the triumph of principles."

Hill's main principle was to work for the end of slavery, and he wanted to be a player in the freedom movement. He told Still that he

---

*King Belshazzar saw the fingers of a man's hand writing on the wall: "Then the king's countenance was changed, and his thoughts troubled him, so that the joints of his loins were loosed, and his knees smote one against another" (Daniel 5:6).

would do for refugees what members of the Vigilance Committee and other abolitionists had done for him: "I will do the best I can for them...." He did admit that some escapees did not thrive in Canada, but it was because "they make no effort."[9]

Hill's wife and children arrived in Toronto at the end of December 1853. She lost her money — about $35 — and went to Niagara Falls and telegraphed her husband to come get his family. Hill wrote Still about the reunion: "We saw each other after so long an Abstance, and you may know what sort of meeting it was, joyful times of corst."[10]

Many of Hill's later letters to Still were about getting friends and relatives out of slavery and about personal matters. On September 14, 1854, Hill wrote Still that their two-year-old son had died. He was clearly saddened, but he was a religious man and came to accept the event because "the almighty God knows what are best for us all." Mrs. Hill did not accept God's will quite that easily: "My wife laments her child's death too much."[11]

Still helped Hill's uncle Hezekiah Hill and brother James Hill escape, Hezekiah going to Canada and James to Boston where it was safe, since he had escaped from Virginia after the Civil War had begun.

According to Still, Hezekiah had tried to buy himself; the price originally quoted was $1,300, but his owner kept increasing the amount. Hezekiah started paying the new figure and had submitted all but $100 of the total when his owner called in a slave trader. Hezekiah immediately ran away in December 1854 from Petersburg to Richmond, where he was hidden under a floor. After 13 months, he and a seven-year-old slave boy, son of the man sheltering Hezekiah, took steamer passage to Philadelphia, where they were helped by the Vigilance Committee.[12]

James Hill, John Henry's brother, was concealed for three years before he escaped. Still does not give details, but the Hills, like Harriet Jacobs, author of *Incidents in the Life of a Slave Girl*, who spent almost seven years secreted in an attic crawl space, were all in hiding before they escaped.

John Henry was interviewed again by the Freemen's Inquiry Committee in the summer of 1863, and references to him were included in Howe's *The Refugees from Slavery in Canada West*, published in 1864.[13]

14. John Henry Hill

He gave an account that is different in some details from what he told Still almost a decade earlier. According to the Howe interview he was born in Virginia in 1835, but 1828 is the year he gave Still. He told Howe that "The whole of our family bought ourselves."[14] In his interview with Still, Hill said he was a runaway. Why did Hill's story change slightly? Slaves often did not know their ages. Also, in 1863 he was an established businessman, and his success would seem even greater if he were younger than he told Still. When he indicated in the Howe interview that family members were hard working and bought their freedom, he was putting himself in the self-help tradition quite different from the civil disobedience tradition of running away.

When Hill was interviewed in 1863, he had three black partners and had established in Hamilton, Canada West, a manufacturing plant processing tobacco grown in Canada West. They secured a building renting for $250 a year, made the wooden parts of their machinery themselves, and employed 20 people, including three white boys. He expected to employ 50 workmen as soon as all the machinery was in place. "We mean to succeed," Hill said, "and we think we shall; for we understand the business and mean to do better work than others do; and merchants will find that out fast enough."[15]

The 1863 commission report emphasized Hill's statement: "The sight of this establishment would astonish those who think negroes too stupid for business, and too lazy for work. It was planned and carried out by colored people, with money of their own earning."[16] The commission then gave an idealized account of the factory where the air must have been heavy from the smell of tobacco and filled with particles of the dried leaves flying from the machinery: "It was marked by the order, silence, and earnestness which pervade all good workshops. There was no talking, laughing, or looking about. Every man was busy at his task.... Each seemed to have the kind of work best suited to him; the men using their brawny arms for lifting and pulling; the boys their tiny fingers for picking and sorting. They were paid in proportion to the worth of their work; and each worked with a will."[17] This description of the activities in a factory is not realistic. The employment of children in a dusty environment was harmful to them. Hill was not responsible, of course, for that romantic picture, but he did employ those children.

Though Hill succeeded as a businessman in Canada, he felt the call of home after the Civil War ended, and he returned to Virginia. Writing in 1872, Still reported that John Henry Hill lived in Petersburg and was justice of the peace. Hezekiah left Toronto for West Point, and James was still living in Boston.[18]

What happened to John Henry and his family as, little by little, blacks were forced back into a segregated society? Did he wish he had stayed in Canada? Unfortunately, we do not know the history of the Hill family after 1872.

15

Mr. and Mrs. John Little

> The fact that there were large tracts of good land in the portion of Canada accessible to the fugitive was a fortunate circumstance, for the desire to possess and cultivate their own land was wide-spread among the escaped slaves. This eagerness drew many of them into the Canadian wilderness, there to cut out little farms for themselves, and live the life of pioneers. The extensive tract known as the Queen's Bush, lying southwest of Toronto and stretching away to Lake Huron, was early penetrated by refugees.
> — Siebert, *The Underground Railroad from Slavery to Freedom*

Mr. and Mrs. John Little, residents of the frontier area known as Queen's Bush, gave extensive interviews to Benjamin Drew for *The Refugee*, published in 1855. Drew began the text of John's interview with high praise: "The hero of the following narrative is much respected, wherever he is known — in Canada West. And in that country of good farms, Mr. Little's is one of the best, and among the best managed."[1] Drew should have praised Mrs. Little also, for John Little knew that his wife was a heroic woman.

In the interviews with the Littles, Drew made clear the differences in their lives in slavery and in free Canada West.[2] Little was born in North Carolina, where he lived for the first 20 years or so with a slaveholder, who was reasonable as far as slave owners went. Little's master owned seven slaves, Little's mother and her six children.

Little's owner fell on hard times and the sheriff seized Little for sale at a public auction. Before the sale, his mother went around to the neighbors wanting one of them to buy her son and thereby keep him near home. All the neighbors refused, for they believed slave traders would pay more than they could. At the auction, Little was sold to a man who lived about ten miles away. He was a gentleman much respected in the community, cruel to his slaves, and known as a "nigger breaker."

Before Little told his story of mistreatment, he made known his views on his second owner: "It don't seem to me that even upon the Lord's day, and now I know there is a hereafter, it would be a sin before God to shoot him, if he were here, he was so bad, he so abused me...."[3] Little was sent to the quarters where about 70 slaves lived. His new life was difficult; the horn woke the slaves early, and they had 15 minutes to get to the home of the overseer. There was no time for breakfast. They worked until after dark. The slaves brought food left over from the night before and ate in the fields when the horses were being fed. They were not allowed to eat at other times during the day. The master gave this order to the overseer: "A nigger could always find time to eat and smoke and shuffle about, and so he wouldn't allow it to us. He wouldn't have his work hindered by eating."[4]

Little put the blame for cruelty against slaves on the master, not the overseer: "No man ought to take the place of overseer, — I blame the scoundrel who takes the office; but if he does take it, he must obey orders."[5] Thoreau expressed a similar thought in "Civil Disobedience" when he wrote with great scorn about order-following marines: "Such a man as an American government can make ... a mere shadow and reminiscence of humanity...."[6]

Little's conflict with his owner, referred to as S — E —, began three weeks after the slave arrived at the plantation. Little had been warned that difficult slaves from the surrounding neighborhood were sent for a year to be forced into submission. S — E — was similar to Mr. Covey, the man who attempted to "break" Frederick Douglass. Douglass wrote that Covey was a poor man, living on rented land, with rented slaves, but with a reputation for controlling recalcitrant slaves. He was also a pious man, a leader in the Methodist church.[7]

Little ignored the warnings about his master. He wanted to see his mother, and asked S — E — on Saturday night for permission to go to see her.

15. Mr. and Mrs. John Little

"No! I don't allow my niggers to run about Sundays, gawking about; I want you to-morrow to look after the mules and the horses along with the rest of the niggers."[8]

Ignoring the order, Little visited his mother without permission, returning Sunday night. The next morning, the overseer and two men of color, presumably Little's fellow slaves, laid hands on him, tied him to an apple tree, and called for the master, who said when he arrived:

"Well, Sir, I suppose you think you are a great gentleman. I suppose you think you can come and go as you please."

"No, I wanted to see my mother very bad and so I ran over there and came back as I told you."

"I am your master, and you will obey me, let my orders be what they may."[9]

S—E—then ordered the overseer to give the disobeying slave 500 lashes. Two slaves then undressed him, pulling his shirt over his head, effectively blindfolding him. Those two slaves were obviously afraid not to follow orders and prepare Little for this extreme punishment. Little could not see what was happening but knew that S—E—was not the one doing the lashing. Before the whipping began, he used his cane to mark Little's body: "Whip him from there down," and the master counted the blows delivered by the overseer. At first, Little was in pain, but by the count of 100 sensation had been beaten out of him.

S—E—then said, "Now, you cursed, infernal son of a b—, your running about will spoil all the rest of my niggers...."

Little announced, "Master, I didn't mean any harm; I wanted to go and see my mother and to get a shirt I left over there." S—E—then struck Little's head with his cane and told the overseer to keep going—"put it on to him again like the very devil."[10]

The overseer continued with a bull whip, and Little did not know how many lashes he received. What he did know was that "from the small of my back to the calves of my legs, they took the skin clear off, as you would skin beef." A slave then washed him with salt water, causing him great misery as his "abominable scoundrel" of a master knew would happen.[11]

Little was then taken to the blacksmith's shop to be put in irons, one of the ways the master used to "break" slaves. Little referred to

S—E—as Satan and said the slaves "were as afraid of him as they would be of a lion out in these bushes."[12] The two slaves in charge of him were admonished to kill him if he tried to escape. They obviously were afraid of S—E—and did not allow Little to disappear into the woods. Little was rigged out with iron rings placed on his ankles with a short chain between them. At night his feet were put in stocks and the ankle bracelets and chain remained in place.[13]

The next day, Little was taken to the cotton gin house where he was to be given 50 strokes with a paddle. After the third strike, he fainted. He was then taken to the field to work but was weak. In the following days, the fetters wore to the bone and his wounds became infected. In spite of mistreatment, Little was stubborn and refused to be beaten into submission. After three months, S—E—had not bought Little under control and decided to send him away.[14]

Little did not dramatize his refusal to be broken as Frederick Douglass did in his *Narrative* published in 1845. Covey at first, through constant whippings and other punishments of Douglass, had the slave broken in spirit, body and soul. After Covey gave him a severe whipping, Douglass went A W O L for a short time. Upon his return he stood up to the slave breaker. Covey at first seemed to be ignoring Douglass' conduct. He sent the slave into the barn to take care of the horses. As Douglass was climbing into the hay loft, Covey tried to tie Douglass' legs together with a rope. Douglass refused to be captured; he jumped down and began to fight Covey. Covey was taken aback by Douglass' resistance. Covey called for a slave named William Hughes to come to his aid, but Douglass kicked Hughes under the ribs, sickening him.

The fight continued, with Douglass saying he was going to continue his resistance. Hughes recovered and Covey asked Hughes for help: "Take hold of him, take hold of him!" Hughes resisted and was disobedient, saying he had been hired out to Covey for work on the farm, not to help punish a slave, and he left the scene. The fight with Covey went on for two hours, with Douglass the winner. For the next six months Douglass served under Covey, the master never once attempted to punish him. This was the rekindling of the idea of freedom for Douglass.[15] Little was not yet at this stage of planning to flee. The slaves of S—E—, unlike Hughes, supported the master.

15. Mr. and Mrs. John Little

Little was sent to Norfolk, Virginia, for shipment to New Orleans. He arrived after the last boat taking slaves for the winter sales in that southern city had departed. Little escaped from jail and returned to the woods near his mother's cabin.[16] He hid out there for the next two years, he told the interviewer. Escaped slaves surviving in the woods or swamps, often near close relatives, was a fairly common occurrence, and capture was also common. S — E — offered $50 for his capture dead or alive, and a free black man betrayed him for $10.[17]

Little was slightly wounded during his capture, was jailed, and was then turned over to a slave driver headed for Tennessee. He was hired out to T — R — in Jackson, Tennessee, and was reasonably satisfied with his master. It was during his years in Jackson that he married. His wife had been born in Petersburg, Virginia. Her family was sold away, and she became the property of old-master's son who treated her well, but his wife was a tyrant. Once a male slave in the house broke a china plate; the mistress threw the pieces at Little's future wife, cutting gashes in four places. She had a scar over her right eye from being hit with a stick of wood. She was once knocked unconscious after his mistress hit her with a pair of tongs. She was, then, abused in slavery, just as he had been. She was 16 at the time of their marriage.[18]

Nine months after the Littles were married, he was jailed and moved to Memphis. He escaped from the planter who was to sell him and started to return to his wife. He was captured, jailed, and fettered. He and another inmate broke out of jail. He found a file in an empty blacksmith shop and removed his chains. Once he rejoined his wife, her master purchased him. Unfortunately, his new overseer relished punishing misbehaving slaves. Mrs. Little learned that her husband was to receive 300 strikes with a paddle. When he came home that night, he was carrying an axe, for he had been chopping timber that day. She had his clothes packed, for she knew he had to flee.

When Mrs. Little told her husband what was to happen to him, he cursed, something he never did, and explained, "If any man, white or black, lays his hand on me to-night, I'll put this axe clear through him — clear through him." The master had a visitor that night, and no one came to the Little cabin. Almost certain violence was averted.[19]

In the meantime, one of the slaves planning to flee with the Littles turned traitor and told the master about the escape plan. The black traitors, Little wrote in a philosophical mood, "are just the same as white men." Little fled.

When it was discovered that Little was missing, the master turned to torture as a means to find the runaway. First, Willis, a slave who was to have escaped with the Littles but had betrayed them, was whipped. Willis did confess that Ohio State was where they were going. A rheumatic boy was whipped but could tell nothing. Next came Mrs. Little. She denied knowledge of escape plans. She was stripped and whipped by a black girl. Mrs. Little pointedly remarked to the interviewer: "Oh, those slave holders are a brutish set of people, — the master made a remark to the overseer about my shape."[20]

Mrs. Little was about 17 when this incident took place, and she was obviously a sexual target. Slave women were aware of the possibility of being sexually abused or raped. Harriet Jacobs in *Incidents in the Life of a Slave Girl* wrote that when she was 15 her master Dr. Flint, 40 years older than she, "began to whisper foul words" in her ear. "He told me I was his property; that I must be subject to his will in all things."[21] She did manage to escape his attentions.

Mrs. Little escaped molestation, but she was whipped with a paddle. She revealed nothing about her husband. Once she was released, she was guarded while the blacksmith made irons for her. The guard was a stupid sort; she told him she needed to get water for the preparation of a meal, he agreed, and she slipped away.[22]

The two Littles met up and fled; they were pursued, with many slaves promised a $10 reward for their capture. The Littles walked nine miles to a town where Little had stored his clothes. Once they retrieved their belongings, they went into a barn, where his exhausted wife fell into a deep sleep. He left for a tavern stable to steal three or four blankets to keep them warm during their travels. Little explained: "If this was wrong, it was taught me by the rascality of my master."[23] Frederick Douglass in his fictional story "The Heroic Slave," has his hero Madison Washington explain thievery in a similar fashion: "The fact is, sir, during my flight, I felt myself robbed by society of all my just rights; that I was in an enemy's land, who sought both my life and my liberty. They had transformed me into a brute; made merchandise of

15. Mr. and Mrs. John Little

my body, and for all the purposes of my flight, turned day into night, — and guided by my own necessities, and in contempt of their conventionalities, I did not scruple to take bread where I could get it."[24]

From the tavern stable where he had just stolen three blankets, Little heard a dog barking and could see a candle burning in the house by the barn. Fearing danger, he hurried to the barn to awaken his wife and escape, but she could not be woken. He put her over his shoulder and ran for a quarter of a mile. Since he was not pursued, he put his wife down and returned to attempt to retrieve his belongings. He then saw the men from the house searching for him. He watched their searches and their attempts to catch him by pretending to have given up the search. Little returned to his wife, who had awakened, and they hid in nearby woods that day. They had a ham with them but ate it raw, as they were afraid that smoke from a fire would give them away. That night he went back and retrieved their things without incident.[25]

The Littles started walking at night and hiding by day. From Jackson, Tennessee, to the Ohio River was 140 miles. Little was afraid to ask for directions, for whites and blacks might betray them for a few dollars. As a result, they often traveled the wrong direction, adding miles to their journey. Her shoes wore out, and she wore his until they came apart. The two walked barefoot the rest of the way to Canada. They faced danger all around them and felt as if they were being hunted like wolves.[26]

The Littles crossed the Ohio River at Cairo, Illinois. Camped on the riverbank, they could hear the bell of a steamboat. To keep the large mosquitoes (she called them "gallinippers") away, they had built a fire, and the smoke blew over to the boat filled with white men, who did not seem to notice the fugitive slaves. Feeling they were safe, the Littles did not douse the fire. Suddenly a yawl boat arrived, and one of the occupants called out, "Boat ashore! boat ashore! runaway niggers! runaway niggers!" The Littles fled to a stand of briars, but without smoke were feasted on by gallinippers. The slave catchers did not find them.[27]

The Littles walked through Illinois, a free state, though there were restrictive Black Laws and many pro-slavery citizens. They met a white woman named Smith, and Little asked if she would sell them some bread, a ploy because what he really wanted was directions. Mrs. Smith said she would give them bread if they came to her house. Once they arrived, Mr. Smith arrived.

"Have you got free papers?"

"No."

"Where are you travelling to?"

"To the upper lakes."

"We are not allowed to let a colored man go through here without free papers; if we do, we are liable to a fine of forty dollars."[28]

Mr. Smith said the Littles could spend the night but the next day would be taken to a nearby justice of the peace; if they were free, they could continue. Mr. Smith seemed sympathetic to the plight of the Littles, but Mrs. Smith said, "If we stop you, we shall get fifty dollars apiece for you; that's a-good-deal-of-money, — you know."[29]

Mr. Smith asked Little if he had a gun, and Little produced his old flint-lock pistol. Smith said he would keep it safe and locked it away. The Smiths lived in a dirty log cabin; they took the mattress off the bed and placed it in front of the only door, preventing the Littles from departing. Smith took his rifle pistol from a cupboard and placed it in reach of the mattress. The Littles slept on the bedstead.[30]

During the night, the Littles made their escape. John Little called out, "Mr. Smith! Mr. Smith! we are unwell and must pass out — we'll be back very soon." Smith pulled the mattress away from the door, and as Little passed Smith's silver-mounted pistol with a percussion lock, he took it. With both amusement and scorn, Mrs. Little told her interviewer: "John has been offered fifteen dollars for it. It the man will come here with John's old flint lock, my husband will exchange and give him boot. I am very sorry for my friend Mrs. Smith, that she did not get the hundred dollars to go shopping with...."[31]

The Littles traveled northward. When they were on the prairie 50 miles west of Springfield, Illinois, they could see a long distance and felt it was safe to walk by day. They reached Chicago, where funds were gathered for them to travel to Detroit, where they crossed into Windsor, Canada West. For the first time in their lives, the Littles were free.

Work was hard to come by in Windsor, and the Littles heard of the sparsely-settled Queen's Bush where "any people might go and set-

15. Mr. and Mrs. John Little

tle, colored or poor, and might have a reasonable chance to pay for the land."[32] They decided to be pioneers, and with only the clothes they were wearing, a quilt and a blanket, and 18 dollars, they were ready. They bought two axes, one for each of them; plates and forks; an iron pot; a Dutch oven; 50 pounds of flour and 20 pounds of preserved pork. In 1841 they literally marched into the wilderness, where, as Little observed, "there were thousands of acres of woods which the [surveyor's] chain had never run round since Adam."[33] As they went into the bush, they faced heavy snow, bears, and wolves. At night they would cut down a tree and build a crude wigwam. They slept on cedar branches.[34]

According to Little, Queen's Bush settlers could claim as much land as they liked, have it surveyed, and pay for it according to quality. The Littles chose the best land and paid $3.70 an acre; originally Little took 100 acres but later added 50 more. In the snow they cut logs for their house and together carried them to the building site, where they lifted them in place. They split cedar logs for shingles. The nearest neighbor was two miles away. Little could not see a white face. In the snow they also began clearing a field, doing all the work without horses or oxen. They had not money for seeds when spring came, but German settlers provided seeds on credit. The Germans priced the seeds and his labor, for the agreement was that Little would help bring in their crops. Though Little is not explicit, the Germans appeared to treat him fairly, something he was not accustomed to. Though it was slow to develop, Little was beginning to lose his distrust, even hatred, of white people.[35]

When the Littles brought in their first crop they had raised 110 bushels of wheat and 300 bushels of potatoes. They had worked together clearing fields, planting, weeding, and harvesting. A little more than a decade later when Benjamin Drew interviewed them for *The Refugee*, the Littles had 110 acres under cultivation, 2 horses, a yoke of oxen, 10 milk cows and young cattle, 20 hogs, 40 sheep, two wagons, and two plows. They were by any standard of the time successful and prosperous farmers.

The Little did receive some help from abolitionists who came to give former slaves in the bush instruction, no doubt about farming methods best suited for the Canadian climate, financial advice, and literacy, which was extremely important because the Littles had been denied education in the United States.[36]

Little came to believe "that it was not the white man I should dislike, but the mean spirit which is in some men, whether black or white."[37]

In the south, Little had been considered a "bad" slave just as Henry Clay's runaway slave Lewis Richardson was.[38] In Queen's Bush, Little could borrow or lend $2,000. Richardson had a chance in a free country, but his life in Canada West is unknown after his stirring speech delivered soon after he arrived.

The British government had allowed Little to live as a free man, and he urged all his fellow men to work against the curse of slavery. He wanted others to see him as a positive example of what a fugitive slave could do when free.

Little had been scarred by his ill-treatment during his years as a slave: "The abuse a man receives at the South is enough to drive every thing good from the mind. I sometimes felt such a spirit of vengeance, that I seriously meditated setting the house on fire at night, and killing all as they come. I overcame the evil, and never got at it — but a little more punishment would have done it."[39]

Mrs. Little does not seem to have been, in her younger years, as vengeful as her husband was. She was abused, but in her interview in *The Refugees* she points with pride to the work she and her husband had done and to their material success. By the time of the interview with Drew, she had a "pleasure-wagon" at her disposal. And at the stores she was treated "as though I were a white woman."[40] That is to say, she was given courteous treatment and called by the title of "Mrs." by merchants and clerks, and clerks would have carried her bulky packages to the wagon.

Mrs. Little paid a cost for her part in their harrowing escape and successful farming on the frontier. She had lost two children — no doubt because of hard work in extreme conditions and poor medical care. Only a daughter, aged four, remained, and she echoed what many free blacks were saying, "I intend to have her well educated, if the Lord lets us."[41]

15. Mr. and Mrs. John Little

As is often the case of working people on farms and those who worked as cooks, maids, barbers, waiters, washerwomen, their lives are too little known. What happened to the Littles after their interview with Drew in 1855 is not known. At that time they were satisfied Canadians, and it is unlikely that they returned to the United States after the end of the Civil War. If tuberculosis, diphtheria, and other life-threatening diseases spared their daughter, she would have been enrolled in school.

Little saw the world from different angles. He had received harsh treatment and was willing to discuss the discontent of slaves. He knew that abusive slave owners could not or should not sleep well at night, because there was always danger that abused slaves might rise up against them, burn their barns, or kill their owners. Though he was free in Canada, Little still felt "the stirrings of revenge."[42]

Little also stressed to Drew that he had a strong work ethic: "I thought I ought to take hold and work and go ahead, to show to others that there is a chance for the colored man in Canada."[43] He succeeded, as Shadrack, the Shadds, the Blackburns, and many others did, but the desire for revenge never left him.

16

Narratives by Refugees in Three Canadian Towns

An Excerpt from
The Refugees: A North-Side
View of Slavery *(1856)*

Benjamin Drew produced a classic study of black refugees in Canada in the 1850s (The Refugee: A North-side View of Slavery, *Boston: John P. Jewett and Company, 1856). Drew traveled to Canadian towns and cities, taking notes on the situation of blacks in that area. We reprint here the final portions of his book: his sections of Amherstburg, Colchester, and Gosfield. Immediately after his introductory paragraphs on the racial situation in each area, he turned to his interviews with the blacks who were living there.*

Drew obviously had begun with a set of questions: Where were you born? Were you born slave or free? If born a slave, how were you treated by your master, mistress, and overseer? How did you escape? If free, why did you come to Canada? How would you describe you life in Canada?

Some refugees answered at length, and there were some especially revealing episodes. In the Amherstburg section, James Smith gives an ironic recollection of a biblical defense of slavery sermon. In the Gosfield section sly Eli Johnson knew that the master had been intimate with slave women and vowed, "If he whips me, I'll put him and his wife in hot water." Johnson's story of how he used this knowledge of sexual misbehavior is a mini–Boccaccio tale. Throughout these stories are accounts of shameful beatings and mistreatments. Many of the refugees seemed

16. Narratives by Refugees in Three Canadian Towns

determined to describe life as a black person in the United States and Canada just as it was. Their accounts, though unverified, have the ring of truth.

The three final sections from Drew's book (pages 245–272) follow.

Amherstburg

Contains a population of more than two thousand. The colored portion is variously estimated at from four hundred to five hundred, — the latter number probably being nearer exactness. Some of these, who had resided in the free States, before emigrating to Canada, assured me that here the colored people are "doing rather better than the same class in the United States."

A separate school had been established here, at their own request: their request was given them, but leanness went with it. I visited the school. There was an attendance of twenty-four, — number on the list, thirty. The school-house is a small, low building, and contains neither blackboard nor chair. Long benches extend on the sides of the room, close to the walls, with desks of corresponding length in front of them. The whole interior is comfortless and repulsive. The teacher, a colored lady, is much troubled by the frequent absences of the pupils, and the miserably tattered and worn-out conditions of the books. Two inkstands were in use, which, on being nearly inverted, yielded a very little bad ink. The teacher appeared to be one of the working sort, disposed to bear up as well as she could under her many discouragements: but the whole school adds one more dreary chapter to "the pursuit of knowledge under difficulties." But there is a better time coming. Malden (Amherstburg) is one of the stations at which the Colonial Church and School Society proposed to establish schools, "expressly for the benefit of the colored race, but open to all."

The colored people are engaged in the various mechanic arts, and as shopkeepers, etc. One of the best hotels is kept by a very intelligent colored man. In an evening walk about town, his was the only house from which I heard the cheerful sound of vocal and instrumental music: and this was occasionally interrupted by some "saucy" white boy shouting, as he passed, a stave of our national, Union-saving air; the same which was played in State street, Boston, by a full band, when Massachusetts swallowed so bitter a dose, that the whole world made up faces: when, with all the pride, pomp, and circumstance of glorious war, it sent one poor "fugitive black man" "to old Virginia's shore." It was all right, no doubt, — for on examining Scriptures, a "passage" from the Constitution, "No person held to service or labor," etc., was found so snugly pasted over Deut. 23:15, that if it were possible, it might deceive the very elect. Therefore, said the people, Burns must be sent back: and the poor fellow was marched off, surrounded by beings who differed mainly from Southern "negro dogs," in not being worth, morally speaking, the remotest approximation to "$100 apiece." It is said that pepper was thrown at them: this was in bad taste, — it had been better to offer them salt — *Turks* Island — as a very useful antiseptic for men who could scarcely boast soul enough to prevent the action of decomposing chemical forces. The reader is requested to pardon this digression, the only one we have made hitherto. It is difficult to speak with calmness when reminded of so disgraceful an action as the surrender of Anthony Burns. The time has come for Americans to adopt the motto of De Witt Clinton — "Patria cara, carior libertas." [Dear is my country, liberty is dearer.]

CHARLES BROWN

I was born in Virginia, and was raised a slave. My grandmother was a free-woman in Maryland. One day, as she was washing by a river, a kidnapper came up, gagged and bound her, carried her into Virginia, and there sold her into bondage. She there had four children, my mother, my mother's sister, and my mother's two brothers. After about twenty or twenty-five years, when I was a very small boy, a man from Maryland, named Hanks, came through Virginia. He saw my grandmother, and knew her. "What!" said he, "are you here?" She told him how she had been kidnapped. He said, "You are free, and I'll get you your freedom." Her oath was good for nothing, but by Hanks's oath, she would get free. At night she was jerked up and carried to Orleans, and sold on a cotton plantation. She wrote on, a good while after, that she would get free, and come back and free her children. She got free herself, as I have heard, but 'twas when she got too old to do any more work. My mother and all the folks there in Virginia knew about her being stolen, and about Hanks's coming there.

I was used kindly, as I always did my work faithfully. But I knew I ought to be free. I told my master one day — said I, "You white folks set the bad example of stealing — you stole us from Africa, and not content with that, if any got free here, you stole them afterward, and so we are made slaves." I told him, I would not stay. He shed tears, and said he thought I would be the last one to leave him.

A year after, I left for the North. I have been cook for large hotels. My health is now very poor, — I have had a bad cough for two or three years, from overwork — cooking sometimes for three hundred persons in a hotel. I have always supported myself, and have some money by me yet. I reside in Chatham, and came here to see a physician.

JAMES SMITH

I was raised on the head waters of the south branch of the Potomac, in Pendleton Co., Va. The treatment there is mild, if there can be any mildness in it. I remained there until my escape in 1847. My father was a white man, and was my master too. My mother's father was also a white man. My master was an Englishman, born in the city of London. When I was five years old, he gave me to his son, who was my half-brother, and he raised me. This son had then children about my age. These children were sent to school, but I was not. These children talked about learning me, but they said, "we musn't — father says he'll write a pass and run off." I have learned to read since I came away. I was ordered about like the other slaves. I ate in the kitchen while they, (my brother's family,) ate at a table by themselves. I was stuck off one side. Other people mentioned my relation to my master, but I never mentioned it to him, nor he to me. His sons had it thrown at them that we favored one another: it was looked on as a stigma. My mother often told me how it was, but told me not to mention it as it would make it worse for her. She died before her master.

My old master was a very wicked man and died a miserable death. My brother was present. My master always had a custom of cursing and swearing, and he died in the same state. Nothing was said about giving me my freedom.

I used to drive to Richmond, and stop at a tavern with white wagoners. I would notice the landlord's countenance, viewing me very much to see if I had colored blood: the wagoners would look at me and wink. They got me in on purpose to joke and bother him. I ate with the other wagoners, excepting a single time. He followed me out into the kitchen where I was eating, and asked me if I was a slave or not. I told him I was. He said I was too white to be a slave. It is often the case that these rascals feel for their own blood—they will say to a man of my color, "It's a pity you're a slave—you're too white to be a slave."

My half-brother got involved and sold me for four hundred dollars to a person in the same neighborhood. I lived with him about two years and six months, clearing up farm six months, balance of the time at grist-mill. His treatment I count well for being a slave. His name was N—E—.

After my father's death, my brothers and sisters, (also my father's children,) four in number, were hired out at auction to the highest bidder. E—came home and told me all about it. I then thought, "I'm doing well enough now, but I don't know how long it will last,—I'll try next fall to get my liberty."

The next fall, I made arrangements and walked away. This was in the fall of '47. After travelling fifty miles, I came right along in the road, and nobody asked me any questions, except one man who knew me, and who proved to be my friend. I stayed upwards of three years in the free States, married there a few days before I left in 1850, and came to Canada. I left the United States, in consequence of the Fugitive Slave Bill—it's only a *Bill*. It vexed me as I was leaving in the boat, to hear the Germans, whom I could understand, laughing about the "niggers" having to leave, and come to Canada. One man was taken away from his wife and three children and carried back before I left.

I am doing tolerably well in Canada, and am getting a very comfortable living. I own a lot of land worth about two hundred dollars, and have other property. I keep a grocery, and sell to all who will buy, without distinction of color.

16. Narratives by Refugees in Three Canadian Towns

THE REV. WILLIAM TROY

From Essex county, Va. My father was a slave of ——, Senator of the United States. My mother was a free-woman.

I lived there until twenty-one. I left there 11th March, 1848. I saw scenes there that made my heart bleed. I can particularize the breaking up of R — P. W —'s farm, some five hundred slaves, many of whom were my associates, with whom I had often been to meeting, belonging to the same church. We had many meetings together, sometimes broken up by patrols. When we had meetings, it was at late hours, to avoid the patrols — yet sometimes they would run us away, and sometimes we would get our meetings through. They were sold to different persons — Judge — and others. About the time a part of them were leaving, I went to bid them farewell. Many had their hearts so full of grief that they could not speak — they could only give me their hands.

Another lot who belonged to the same man, aroused me by singing about nine at night, passing my father's residence, singing, bidding farewell to all their friends; many left father, mother, and children behind them. I may mention here that one of these slaves, a woman named Martha Fields, who was hired out at the time, was taken early one morning, without time to get her clothes, hurried off to Richmond, and sold to the highest bidder. From Richmond she went on to New Orleans, put into a slave-pen, and bought by Mr. A —, a celebrated negro trader, and put on his farm, where she married A.'s slave. A. gave them free papers, and they now reside in Cincinnati. She says she has suffered enough herself, and seen so much suffering, that she believes that all those who hold slaves, and those who uphold slavery will, if there is any such place as one of torment, will be sure to go there.

I was aroused at Loretto, Va., by the sale of a slave named William, who was sold by his master. I heard the boy hollowing in the swamp; from hearing his shrieks, I made towards the boy, — when I went there, I found him in the act of catching the boy to have him sold. His mother, who grieved much at the sight, was told if she did not hush, her back would be cow-hided. This same man, soon after that, took her into the stable to whip her, and finding some difficulty about getting off her clothes, took his knife and cut them from her, and whipped her until she bled. Before I came away, he had sold the last one of her children. This man was N — S —.

These are facts which cannot be denied by the persons whom I have named, and I intend to be a terror to the system while I live.

Personally, I have suffered on account of my color in regard to education. I was not allowed to go to school publicly, — had to learn privately. The reason of my coming away was, I knew that I was open to the assaults of any ruffian, if he were a white man, and if I made any reply, I was liable to nine and thirty before what they call a justice of the peace. Further, I could not educate my children there, and make them feel as women and men ought — for, under those oppressive laws, they would feel a degradation not intended by Him who made of one blood all the people of the earth.

I have been here a few weeks only — am settled as pastor over the First Baptist Church; about one hundred usually attend divine service here, most of whom have been slaves. They seem to enjoy religion and freedom very much indeed. None are desirous to return to the corn-cobs of Egypt.

At Enorn Church, Essex county, Va., colored and white meet together. On the first Sabbath in the month the colored assemble with the white pastor to attend to their church business after sermon. Sometimes a few whites are present on this Sabbath. I used to go to church regularly, but never heard them preach from, "Masters, render unto your servants that which is just and equal:" but I will write down as near as I can, (and I recollect all his points,) a sermon preached by Rev. Mr.—, on the first Sabbath in the month, and the church proceedings.

Sermon Preached at the Baptist Church Called Enorn,
by the Rev. Mr.—

> Eph. 6:5. Servants, be obedient to them that are your masters according to the flesh, with fear and trembling, in singleness of your heart as unto Christ.
>
> First, — Let me state relative to the different positions we occupy in life: I am not a lawyer, neither am I a senator, nor a judge of any court, — still I am contented, because Providence has placed me so, and I am will-

ing to submit to his Divine will; and the Apostle tells us, that godliness with contentment is great gain.

Secondly, — Now, you brethren that suffer affliction, should endure it as good soldiers, enduring all hardness. Paul says to his son Timothy, "Let as many servants as are under the yoke count their own masters worthy of all honor, that the name of God and his doctrine be not blasphemed." And they that have believing masters, let them not despise them. These are holy injunctions, and must be adhered to. Be contented under all circumstances with singleness of heart to God, not giving railing for railing, but with fear do the will of your master. Count not your slight affliction dear, for God your Father hath so decreed from all eternity that you should suffer, and if you despise the imposition of God, you cannot enjoy his spiritual benefits.

Again, — we will have to take into consideration the base action of one of our brethren who ran away from his master. When we go into this work, you must consider the obligation that the servant is under to his master; then examine the text, and you will know that we shall be compelled to excommunicate brother Reuben Smith for running away from his master, Mr.——.

Now the Deacons (colored) who are present will state the case, and we will take action on it. Deacon R—, you will state what you know about Reuben's running away.

Deacon R. Yes, Sir; I know that he ran away from his master, and so far as I know about such conduct, I believe it wrong, and can't be tolerated by us.

Minister. Will Deacon Edmund—, come forward? State what you know about the case.

Deacon E. It is true, Sir, that Reuben ran away, and we must exclude him for it.

Minister. Now, brethren, you hear the statements of your deacons, what will you do with the case?

Deacon R. I move that we exclude brother Reuben, for running away from master.

Deacon E. I second that.

Minister. All that are in favor of that motion will hold up your right hand. It is unanimous. Well, brethren, we have done God's will, let us sing and conclude our meeting. Billy, will you sing?

> "Jerusalem, my happy home!
> Oh, how I long for thee!
> When will my sorrows have an end,
> My joys when shall I see?"

Receive the benediction.— May the God of peace crown our efforts with success, and save us all in the end, for the Redeemer's sake. Amen.

Reuben Smith was a preacher, and an intelligent man: that's the reason he ran away. He was caught in the city of Washington, and sold into Louisiana.

WILLIAM LYONS

I have worked in Amherstburg at joining — have worked here two years. I get 15s. York, a day. My family are in Detroit. I was free-born in Virginia, and have been ill-treated in the free States, on account of my color. I went into Columbus, Ohio, to work at my trade; I was employed in a shop. The journeymen all left the shop — wouldn't work in the shop with a colored man — wouldn't think of it. I persevered, and got employment from one who defied the prejudice of the city, — Mr. Robert Reardon. After that I found no difficulty at all, and was treated like a gentleman. The people there who had employed me wished me to remain. I own property there now.

The colored people here are industrious and doing well. They are doing as well as those in the States. There is less whiskey drinking by colored people here, than in any place I know of. They use less, in my opinion, than the whites in general.

JOSEPH SANFORD

At 10 years old I was moved to Kentucky, from Madison Co., Va. I remained in Kentucky till about 50.

My father always advised me to be tractable, and get along with the white people in the best manner I could, and not be saucy. My mother always taught me to serve the Lord — which had ever been my aim; in which I am not the least tired, and am more anxious to go forward than ever. I could almost lay down my life for an abolitionist, for had it not been for them I should have been in slavery still. I believe the Lord will bless them. They have done every thing for me, and it makes my soul melt towards them.

I recollect that my master in Virginia was a monstrous bad man, but not half so bad as some others. I recollect that my mother wanted some salt to put into bread. My mistress, whenever we came down stairs, would search our pockets, to see if we had taken any thing. I went up to get some salt for my mother, and put half a pint in my

16. Narratives by Refugees in Three Canadian Towns

pocket. My mistress said, "Let me feel you pocket!" I was afraid and ran. She called her son to catch me, as I had got something. He caught me and punished me very heavily with a cowhide — he beat me till I was out of breath.

In Kentucky, after a few years, the old man died, — I fell to one of his daughters — she hired me out to a brother-in-law. She was very good to me. I was hired out eight years to different persons. My mistress then died. She wanted me to be set free. Some of her kinsfolks said no, — that her brother had had bad luck, and she had better will me to him. She, being bad off, being sick, and not knowing how to carry her mind, — she did so: she willed me to her brother. He kept me seven years working on the farm. He was going to move into Campbell Co. I had a wife and four children. To leave me, he swapped me for another man. I lived with him about thirteen years. He was a very clever man. He was pretty rich — a sportsman, gambler, horse-racer, etc. He came to get broke. Then we were seized and sold. J — G — bought me. My master was now a most cruel man. There was a great many who had a high regard for me. I was respected by everybody — could be trusted, no matter with what. I used to do his marketing, going to Cincinnati, sell his butter, flax-seed, potatoes, apples, peaches, yarn — every thing — and took every copper home. I wanted to be free, but was afraid to undertake it; for I thought if I were taken and carried back, it would be a great disgrace to me, as I was always trusted. They thought no more of trusting me with fifty or sixty dollars in their stores than with half a dollar. I made enough raising tobacco nights and Sundays to come to more than seventy or eighty dollars a year. I had always been trusty, and had been foreman on the farm.

My master concluded that he must get an overseer. The overseer made the bargain, that he was not to interfere with the hands at all — what he wanted, he was to go to the overseer, who was to order the hands. The overseer carried on very well. He kept us moving from Monday morning until noon, Saturday — then we left work until Monday. This did not suit master nor mistress — it was a little too much privilege. If the fourth of July or a holday was a Friday we had it, and Saturday afternoon as before. This troubled my master more than ever. He began to get very uneasy. I had not had a whipping for twenty years, and I said if they would put a hand on me, that I wouldn't stop any longer. The overseer observed, that he had made a rule that three boys were to make a turn about, one one Sunday, and another the next, to see things correct on the place. I had a wife at home, and was there more or less every Sunday. I always wanted to go to meeting: sometimes I would stop after meeting, but was always at home early to do the business.

The next Sunday after, the overseer was not satisfied, because none of us had stayed at home. He called me down to the barn, — he had a cow-hide under his coat. He said, why didn't you stay at home yesterday? I told him I wanted to go to church, and came home in the afternoon, after the church was out. "I told you to stay at home," said he, "and whatever I tell you to do, you've go to do it." The whipping he gave me did not hurt me so much as the scandal of it, — to whip so old a man as I was, and who had been so faithful a servant as I had been: I thought it unsufferable. This was about the time the year rolled round. The overseer's time was out, and the master took his place. I don't suppose I could tell in two hours what I went through.... In the spring about the 1st of May, he had the corn ground broken up completely. Planted the corn, three of us, fifty acres. After it came up we ploughed in it before holiday. I worked hard to try to please my master. He came home and asked me, "Where have you been ploughing?" "Such and such a piece." "Is that all you've ploughed?" I told him it was. "Well," says he, "I could plough more land in one day, than you and Dave both have ploughed." It was as big a lie as ever was told, but I did not dare contradict him. The same day, he started away to buy up cattle. "Now," says he, "I'll tell you what you've got to do: you've got all this field to weed out, replant, chop all the big briers out, then go to the high-tower place, weed out that, chop out all the big briers and replant it: then go down to old Archy Rendle, and do the same there." "I can't do that," says I, "to-day and to-morrow." "I don't tell you to do it to-day and to-morrow," said he, "you've to do it against I come back, if you don't I'll thump you." He told Ben and Dave to plough the same fields over with two furrows in a row. Monday was holiday; but he said, "you must go into Monday too:" taking away our holiday, which was never done to me before.

16. Narratives by Refugees in Three Canadian Towns

Finding that he was going to take away our holidays, — we all resolved to break and run away, hit or miss, live or die. There were thirteen of us started away in company, — not all from his place. One of the boys went down to Covington and made the arrangements. On a Sunday night we made our break, and when we got to Covington, it was daybreak; the garrison were up, beating their drums. God was on our side, or we should have been gone. We divided at the last toll-gate. Some going through the gate and myself and little Henry going round. We then found a skiff and oars, got in the skiff and crossed the Ohio into Cincinnati. I was so afraid I'd see somebody that knew me, I knew not what to do. When I got up on Main St., I saw a great black smoke coming out of the chimney of a steamboat as if she was coming right across, — I was certain she was coming after me. I met draymen who say, "Are you travelling?" "No, I'm going up on the hill, to see my brother." My wife was nearly about to give out. "Joe," said she, "do pray stop a few minutes and let us rest." Said I, "I cannot stop, — if you want to stop you can, but I must go on." I caught her by the arm, and helped her on to the top of the hill. There I met a friend —

[Mr. Sandford's narrative was here interrupted. The concluding portion is luckily supplied, however, in the narrative that follows.]

JOHN HATFIELD

I am a native of Pennsylvania; and a mulatto. I was employed as a barber on a steamboat plying from New Orleans to Cincinnati. At one time, while in New Orleans, I was afraid they would take me under the law, and put me in jail. I would not conceal myself on board the boat, but went up and stayed with a friend, until I thought it time for the boat to start. But I was too soon, and came back to the boat the day before she sailed. I was arrested, ironed in the street to degrade me, and put in the jail, where I remained twenty-three hours. I found in the jail men from Boston, New York, Baltimore, and other places. There was a chain-gang in there rattling, one crazy fellow shouting — it was awful! It reminded me of the place of torment more than any thing else. In the morning the whip was cracking, starting out the chain-gang, just as one would start up horses. They measured me, and recorded my name. I had committed no crime. I never felt so degraded in my life. If I had murdered a man or stolen a horse, I could not have been treated with more contempt. A friend of mine sent a bed to the jail for me to sleep on — they would not take it in, — said I had a good bed — it was a plank and a blanket. They fed me on baked beans and pork, and charged me eleven dollars. It was a complete system of robbery. They make thousands of dollars so, out of the poor colored people. Still New Orleans used to be the best place in the Union for colored people, after they got the right of citizenship: but I am told it is getting to be harder on them now.

I was in Cincinnati when thirteen slaves reached there, running from Kentucky. They got there at seven or eight in the morning. They were questioned very closely by slave-catchers. One, pretending to be their friend, put them in a cellar, and was guarding them very closely, in order to get the reward. Among the slaves were Joseph Sanford and his wife. A few of us hearing of it, went there as quick as possible, and found the man stopping up the holes in the cellar to keep people from seeing them. I went in and asked Mrs. Sanford if she knew that man. She said, "No — never saw him before." I said, "You must get out of this." I put a comrade to watch the man, and we took them out two at a time, and hid them in various parts of the city. Their pursuers were there in less than an hour. They offered large rewards to any one who would just tell what square they were in. But the rewards would not fetch them: a million of dollars would not take a slave in Cincinnati out of some people's hands.

They stayed concealed a fortnight, and then myself and others guided them on the way to Michigan, which they reached in safety. However, they were afterwards all captured in Michigan: but they got off before a judge, and were then sent over the line into Canada.

I came into this country on account of the oppressive laws of the United States. I have as good friends in the United States, colored and white, as even a man had, — I never expect to get so good friends again — but the *laws* were against me.

I never felt better pleased with any thing I ever did in my life, than in getting a slave woman clear, when her master was taking her from Virginia. She came on board a steamboat to Cincinnati. She had got to a friend's house in the city. Word came to my ears that too many knew where she was. I went there and told the friend; he thought she was safe. Then I went home about sundown from there, and about dark he came to me—he told me they had been there,—they came to the back door,—he wrapped her in a blanket, took her out of a front window, and took her across the street. A man asked him what he had there. "A sick man." He took her to another friend's house across the street: that house was next surrounded. I took a young man's clothes (he lived at my house) and dressed her in them,—we came out at a gate near by, we crossed over the street;—there were five or six persons then coming towards us—all I could say was, "walk heavy!" for they came right upon us. They walked with us half a square—I was scared only for her. They stopped a little—we got fifty yards ahead of them. I then told her, "they are coming again,—hold your head up, and walk straight and heavy!" By this time they were up with us again: they walked with us a whole square, looking right in her face, trying to recognize her. We came to where there was a light opposite,—I turned the corner and said, "Come this way, Jim." She understood, and followed me. Upon this, they turned and walked away as fast as they could walk. What I said *had the effect*. I put her in a safe place, and took a turn back again: I wanted to have some fun. There were about a dozen standing at the corner, near the house where they supposed she was, talking about it. I went into a corner house,—there were several of us in there, and we went to laughing and talking about it: we did this on purpose to make fun of them. They went away to a house, and said they had seen the "nigger" dressed in men's clothes, but that they were afraid to take her, there were so many "niggers" round. There was no one with her but me, but they did not want to have it appear they were beaten so badly. We had a good deal of sport out of it,—the woman we called "Jim," as long as she stayed there. She came to the North at last. I have had fifteen runaways harbored in my house at one time—in one year, twenty-seven.

Colchester

This beautiful farming town, on the northern shore of Lake Erie, contains a population not far from 1,500, of whom about 450 are colored persons.

The reeve of the town, Peter Wright, Esq., informed me that much of the land which has been opened to cultivation was cleared by fugitive slaves. They leased portions of wild land for a term of years, and by the time they had made a good clearing, they were obliged to go somewhere else. The amount of crime among them was no more than might have been expected from so ignorant and unenlightened a people. But as a whole, there is a manifest improvement in respect to honesty, and in their general deportment.

They have the same opportunity to instruct their children as is enjoyed by the whites, — that is, they draw their share of the school funds, and the trustees are bound to employ competent teachers. It would be convenient sometimes to employ teachers from the United States, but in that case they cannot draw government money.

The fugitive slave bill drove into Canada a great many who had resided in the free States: these brought some means with them, and their efforts and good example have improved the condition of the older settlers.

The town clerk of Colchester coincided in the main with Mr. Wright, but expressed himself in more positive terms on the general improvement of the colored race. They have, however, I fear, but few friends among the white settlers. "They ought to be by themselves;" "if we try to encourage them, we shall have to mix with them," — these and similar expressions are very common. There are not many who wish to see the colored people come up to an equal rank with themselves, politically or otherwise. The True Bands even begin to form an object of groundless distrust.

Mr. Benj. Knapp, a native of the town, an intelligent farmer, and who is one of the assessors, gave me some information, which, with a few items from other sources, and the statements of the colored people themselves, will show the state of things in Colchester.

The school system is not so well organized as in some of the States, sectarianism and prejudice interfere too much: the law allows too many separate schools paid for out of the public funds.

The front part of the township along Lake Erie is well cleared up. The farms in this part belong to white settlers, native Canadians. In the interior there is yet a great deal of wild lands: to clear these up must be a work of time. Back of the cleared farms on the Lake shore, are farms owned mostly by whites, as far back as the fourth concession, with here and there a farm owned by a colored man. These farms are not generally so thoroughly not so neatly cultivated as those of the whites; though there are some white men's farms no better than theirs.

In regard to fugitives, there is not one who cannot find work within a few hours after he gets here. There is no trouble about that: "we can't get men enough to do our work."

Beyond the fourth concession, "farms belonging to white and colored are mixed in." This is a newly settled part; it is within a few years that farmers have begun to settle there. Colored people have penetrated further into the woods than any of the whites: they are scattered all through the township up to the sixth concession. They are settled both north and south of the old Malden road: none would have ventured there but them: they are all anxious to own land: they go in anywhere they can make a claim, and clear up a patch. But their ignorance stands most wofully, and in some cases insurmountably, in their way. Instances of this sort are said to have occurred: a settler for instance takes a farm of 100 acres, appraised value $200, with ten years to pay for it in. He pays $12 a year *interest* for ten years, supposing meanwhile that he is paying up the principal. *He do n't understand it,*— and when the ten years have come round, he had not got the $200, and must leave his clearing.

The colored people send their children to school, when they have schools, and seem anxious to send their children to school. The "Colonial Church and School Society" have noted this town as a school station.

The settlement spoken of above where the colored people have "penetrated into the woods," is known as New Canaan. It is a prosperous settlement, in which the element of progress is strikingly manifest.

Robert Nelson

I was born in Orange county, Va. My mother was sold away from me before I can remember. I was taken from Virginia at seven, and remained there in Kentucky, in Boone county, until forty-seven. While

I was in slavery, I belonged to a man who used me as he did his children, except that he gave me no education. I cannot write or read.

My master got involved, and I was mortgaged. The mortgage was out and closed, — the sheriff got after me, and I ran to Canada. I was to have been taken to a cotton farm in Louisiana. This was in April, 1845. I left without money. I had heard about the abolitionists, but was afraid of them: I thought no white men would do what they said the abolitionists would do. I had been told that they would sell us. So I was afraid to trust them. The abolitionists wanted to have a meeting to raise money for me, but I slipped out of their hands. After I got here, I found they were all true.

Some persons who wanted to betray me, told me I could not live in Canada. I came in without a shilling. I now own a house and one hundred and one acres of land. I have averaged about fifteen acres of land a year that I cultivated, having myself two thirds of the crop. This enabled me to support myself and family, and buy land. My wife belonged to another man. I sent on and bought her for $400.

It is reported throughout the world, that colored people cannot live here: I have been here ten years, and have seen no one starving yet. Any man that will work can get $10 or $12 a month, cash, and more if he takes it in trade. I can raise corn sixty or seventy bushels to the acre, as good corn as ever was raised in the South. It has been stated that the colored population are lazy, and won't work. The principal part all work. This report has been got out by begging agents, to fill their own pockets by raising money.

The prejudice is higher here in this place than in any part of Canada. It arises from a wish to keep the colored people so that they can get their labor. They used to work for the whites, but they only received half price, and cases have been known where, for ten pounds of pork, the laborer received five. The fugitive, as ignorant of figures as a hog is of holiday, had cunning enough to go to another place and get it weighed. By these means, the colored people became unwilling to work for the whites, and tried to make themselves independent. They began to take up land and work for themselves: of course the whites could not hire them. They have consequently become freeholders, and are of some consequence at the polls.

16. Narratives by Refugees in Three Canadian Towns

The colored people have cleared up two thirds of what has been cleared in this township. Those who came first, bought lands of individuals and lost them again: but when they began to buy of the government, they began to have good claims on the land.

Some, when they first came, would take a lease of a few acres of wild land, for six or seven years. By the time they had got it cleared, and removed some of the stumps, the lease was out. Then the white man said, "you can't have that piece any more, — you must go back in the bush." They found they must do different from this. They began to work on the land for themselves, and to get farms of their own. Now because the white men cannot hire them, they say the colored people won't work.

They say, too, that the colored people steal. It may be that a few are a little light-fingered, they take, perhaps, a few small articles, and the greatest mischief is, it scandalizes us. What two or three bad fellows do, prejudice lays to the whole of us. But some white men have stolen on the credit of the colored. It is very easy to say when a thing is missed, — "O, 'tis some colored man stole it," — although, it has, to my knowledge, been proved, that when theft was charged on a colored man, it turned out that a white man did it.

There is a settlement here called New Canaan, where was a large body of wild land. Colored people went in and took it up at one hundred acres apiece. I guess there may be now forty families. [In 1852, there were twenty families.] They paid the first instalment, and had ten years to pay in. But three quarters of them have already paid the whole price, and got the deeds, and are making good improvements on their lands, making enough to support their families. The preaching of the gospel is regularly kept up.

My wish to the people of the States is, to give no more money to the begging agencies. If they wish to give money to the fugitives and the sick, it should be given to the True Band societies, who can disburse it as it is wanted. The Band will attend to the fugitives.

David Grier

I was born free in Maryland, — was stolen and sold in Kentucky, when between eight and nine years old. In Kentucky I was set free by will, and as they were trying to break the will up, some of my claimant's friends persuaded me to come off to Ohio. From Ohio, I came here on account of the oppressive laws demanding security for good behavior, — I was a stranger and could not give it. I had to leave my family in Kentucky.

I came in 1831. I have cleared land on lease for five or six years, then have to leave it, and go into the bush again. I worked so about thirteen years. I could do no better, and the white people, I believe, took advantage of it to get the land cleared. This has kept me poor. I guess I have cleared not short of seventy or eighty acres, and got no benefit. I have now six acres cleared.

Ephriam Waterford

I was born free; was bound until twenty-one, in Virginia. The man I was bound out to, was to teach me to read and write, but did not — never gave me any education at all.

I came into Indiana in the spring that James K. Polk was made President. I stayed there till about two years ago. I left on account of oppression in Indiana. I had a farm there of forty acres paid for, and I had the deed. A law was passed that a colored man could not devise real estate to his wife and children, and there were other equally unjust laws enacted. I told them "if that was a republican government, I would try a monarchical one." Between thirty and forty of us, little and big, came over at the same time. I have a farm here of two hundred acres wild land: I have five acres under fence in corn now. E. Casey and S. Casey came over at the same time. They are doing first-rate. Both have farms on the 1st concession — I think between twenty-five and thirty acres under fence together.

There is prejudice right smart in some places in this town. We try to live as upright as we can, get a little stock, etc. The whites can easily hire any colored man who has no work to do for himself. A great many are doing hired work about the town to-day — hired more by white men than by colored, and white being more able. I intent to give my child an education as I can.

16. Narratives by Refugees in Three Canadian Towns

ELI ARTIS

I have twenty-five acres of land, bought and paid for, — about eight acres cleared. I am often hired out, and never refuse to work where I can get my pay, and have often worked when I got no pay. The colored people are industrious, and if any say they are not willing to work, it is a lie, and I'll say so, and sign my name to it.

I sufferer from mean, oppressive laws in my native State, Ohio, or I would not have been in this country. I have lived here fourteen years.

EPHRAIM CASEY

I am from the State of Georgia, where I was born free. But the laws were not better about learning for a free man than for a slave. I was never sent to school in my life. My opportunities for religious information were poor. I am now a member of the Methodist Church. At about twenty-three, I emigrated to Indiana, carrying no property. In Indiana, I attended to farming. I had a farm there, and when I left, owned one hundred and eighteen acres. I left on principle — on account of the laws. I like the country very well. The laws bore hard on me before I came away — I had a case in law, and could not prove my side good by the evidence of colored men, which caused me a loss of fifty or sixty dollars. I did not feel disposed to stand this, and emigrated into Canada.

I settled in Colchester, where I bought out a white settler, land and stock, for seven hundred and fifty dollars. The farm was sixty acres, one half improved: seventeen head of hogs, and five head of cattle. There was no good water there. He had dug in a few places, but got no supply. I sunk a well twenty-eight feet, and the water now rises and runs over the surface, a stream eighteen inches deep; enough to supply water for a steam saw-mill. I have growing eight or ten acres of corn, five or six in wheat, two or three in oats, some potatoes, and other vegetables. The land is better than where I was in Indiana.

I moved in, two years ago last May. I have hired colored men to work for me whenever I wanted their help, and have seen them hired by others: but they prefer, so far as I know, to work for themselves, and to get an independent living.

Rev. William Ruth

I am a native of Bourbon county, Ky., left there at twenty-seven, and have resided principally in Colchester since 1825.

I never met with any rough usage in slavery. It was expected that I would be set at liberty at thirty-one, by the will of my former master; but as there was supposed to be a disposition not to give me a fair chance, I was assisted off by a man who was a slaveholder himself. There are a great many such movements there.

I was young when I left there, but often saw separations of families by sales and by hiring. I happened to fall to an Irishman, who was a good sort of a man — an extraordinary man for a slaveholder — in advance of all the country for kindness to his slaves.

I have fifty acres of land under fence, and had it all cleared and improved years ago. It is well supplied with water. I have an orchard with a good assortment of fruits — apples, pears, and peaches. It is one of the best farms in Colchester. I own seventy acres besides in New Canaan.

New Canaan is going to be one of the finest and most beautiful places. It has every advantage necessary to make it a fine settlement. It is covered with heavy timber, and has a first-rate soil. The settlers are doing extraordinarily for the time they have been there.

The colored people have their inferior class as well as other people; I mean a careless, loafing, negligent, vicious class — and they have their turn in prison, like other persons of that sort. We don't claim to be better than other people, but we claim to be as good.

In regard to education, we are destitute of it, as a general thing. But the prospect is advancing. The government schools are kept up. The rising generation are improving.

My candid opinion in regard to raising money in the United States for fugitives is, that they should have an agent here whom they can place confidence in, and have him expend it under the direction of a committee of white men belonging to the province. I would have the board white, in order to bring the races more to an understanding and better feeling towards each other; another reason is, that the colored population have not generally had the opportunity to learn how to transact business. They might, as they improve, be placed on the board.

16. Narratives by Refugees in Three Canadian Towns

The society over which I am placed, is connected with the Wesley or New Connexion in Canada. I preach every Sabbath, generally two or three times a day. They pay good attention to religion, and as a general thing are a moral people. The laws of chastity are well observed: in this they excel the whites.

Gosfield

Numbers nearly 2,600 inhabitants. The whole colored population, by actual count, is 78.

Of the heads of families, all but two or three are freeholders, and some of them have very good farms. James King, Esq., Clerk of the Courts for the County of Essex, C. W., thus characterized the colored people of Gosfield: "They are good, loyal subjects, and good, honest people. They are as moral as any people. There is no fault to be found with them at all."

JOHN CHAPMAN

I was originally from Kentucky, but removed into Indiana at fourteen. I did not feel safe in Indiana, and removed with my family into Canada at Gosfield. Then it was pretty much all bush. The farmers raised but little more than they wanted themselves. One raises as much now as twenty did then. It was hard to get a start when I came to this country.

There are now seventy-eight men, women, and children: when I came there were but three colored. We live like rich folks, but when we came I was almost discouraged.

They are generally getting along as well as could be expected. All make a good living. Most of them own houses and land. They generally attend divine service, and sent their children to school when it is open. It is not kept up in the summer.

THOMAS JOHNSON

I was raised in Virginia, which I left with my master for Kentucky, at the age of twenty-one. Twenty years after we moved, my master died, and I remained with my mistress taking care of the farm. I used to take a great deal of care of the place, seeing to the farming operations, and have been to Cincinnati to sell produce. The people all considered me trustworthy and honorable, and some of the white people said I could make greater crops than they could.

I had a wife and several children on a neighboring farm. She wished to leave for Canada, with the three youngest children. I gave her money and she got away into Canada safe enough. As soon as she was gone, I was seized and put in jail — her owners said, if they shut up the hen they could soon find the chickens. They asked me in the jail, "if I knew she was going?" I asked them "if they knew the height and size of my wife?" They said they did. "Well," I told them, "that is my life — and if your wife has done as many pretty things for you, as mine has for me, wouldn't you be willing to give her a little money to help her?" In a few days, I was let out. I still continued on the farm attending faithfully to my work — but my mistress' friends, suspecting that when she died, I would run off to rejoin my wife, persuaded her to sell me. One day, eighteen months after my wife left, I was sent for to the house. I went in, and asked my mistress what was wanting. "Oh dear!" said she, "I don't know, Thomas." But I know what 'twas for. Said I, "When our Savior was on earth, they could make out nothing against him, till they got false witnesses, — and there are false witnesses against me."

I was kept at the house that night, in charge of three men, but was not put into strict confinement. The next morning, one of them produced a pair of handcuffs connected with a long chain, and said, "we must put these on, Thomas." I said, "You will not put them on to me, — I have done nothing for which I should wear such things as them." "I'll tell you the truth, Thomas," said he, "we are going to send you down the river."

I was sitting at the grunsel, and as I sat, I carefully slipped off my boots, then jumped up and ran for the woods. They ran after me a short distance. I had thirty-five dollars in my coat pocket, which came in the way, running. I held it up in my hand, and as I did so, turned to look behind me. My mistress' son was at a fence, and he sometimes less, — must be on hand else got the whip. If there was deemed sufficient

16. Narratives by Refugees in Three Canadian Towns

cause, if there was any word, or the least thing they did not like, the man was staked down for four hundred lashes. I saw a man staked down and whipped one Sunday, until the blood lay in a pool on each side of him. It was through the fear of the Lord, that I endured the persecution put upon me, — I suffered a great deal there, — and but for the fear of the Lord and the worth of my own soul, I should have murdered the overseer. When I first went it was a warm climate: I had to drink the muddy water of the river, which made me sick and weakened me down. Every day I was threatened with seven hundred and fifty lashes, if I complained of being sick. I had to keep on: being of strong constitution I began to mend, and endured all they put on me for six years.

My wife was with me, and was made to suffer worse than I. I was in constant fear of the lash, but made out to plead off, although the whipping seemed to be sometimes, just to keep their hand in. Many men and women were punished with a paddle and whip. I had to make paddles with twelve holes in them. A block lay in the cotton yard over which they were placed to be paddled. I saw them take one man and paddle him, then they struck him with a handsaw, then with a bull whip: then they ordered me to lock the biggest log chain I could find on the place around his neck with the biggest lock, and keep him at my house until next morning. I went out in the field leaving him at the house, not believing him able to get out. The overseer gave me so many minutes to go and get him. I went back for him, and met him hobbling along with the chain. He had to work at chopping wood. Three weeks he wore the chain: then myself and another bailed him, and the chain was taken off: if he had run away, we were to wear the chain. Three days after the whipping, he was allowed no food. We gave him some of ours, but did not dare let it be known.

The whipping was because he ran away. He ran away, because the overseer appropriated his wife. The man threatened to do something about it, — the overseer threatened him with a whipping, — then he ran away. I know all this, — I saw the treatment with my own eyes. E — was the overseer's name, — he stayed there three years.

While under E —, I was put on short allowance of food and made to work on the Sabbath, etc. I was then a professor and used to hold prayer-meetings Saturday night. One Saturday night, during meeting, E — sent for me. I went to him. He told me to stay until he had eaten breakfast next morning, then he would stake me down and give me five hundred lashes; for he wouldn't have such things as meetings carried on. I managed to slip off, and went to the cabins. I went back to him next morning while he was at breakfast: his wife was facing me, he was back to me. She pointed at me, and said, "there he is." I clapped my hands together and said, "In the name of God why is it, that I can't after working hard all the week, have a meeting on Saturday evening? I am sent for to receive five hundred lashes for trying to serve God. I'll suffer the flesh to be dragged off my bones, until my bones stare my enemy in the face, for the sake of my blessed Redeemer." He did not come to me, — he appeared startled at my appearance. He went into the house from the porch, got his gun and walked away. After he had gone I walked away.

I think the reason he did not punish me was, that once when it got to me that he said he would whip me, and his wife wished he would, I had said, — "If he whips me, I'll put him and his wife in hot water." I knew that he had been intimate with some of the slave women. He told me at one time to leave my cabin door, so he could get in, in the night, on account of one of two girls that were there. I left the door on the latch, and warned the girl. He came — but she struggled against him, got away, and came to the bed where were I and my wife. His wife heard what I said about "hot water," and sent for me, making an excuse about a partition. She placed a chair near me, "Well, Eli," she says, "what's that you was going to put me and my husband in hot water for?" I tried to turn it off. She insisted, and at last got mad because I wouldn't tell her, and said she'd make him make me tell. He made her believe, that he would make me tell, and he told me that he wouldn't for his right arm have his wife know. So I knew what grounds I stood on, and kept clear of the lash.

The next overseer was S —. He kicked a woman's eye out, the first day he came there. He asked her a question in the gin-house, which she did not understand. She said "No, Sir," at a venture. The answer was wrong — she was stooping down, and he kicked her face. It put her eye out. He went to the house for something to put one it. She cried out aloud. Said he, "Shut up! I've killed a great many better looking niggers than you, and thrown 'em in the bayou." This I heard him say myself. Nothing was done about the loss of the eye: the woman's husband dared say nothing about it. In three weeks' time, S— whipped three women and nine men. The talk in the quarters was among some to put him to death; others were afraid to try it. He left before the month was up; another named W— was then overseer.

He went on rather roughly. There had been an underhanded business done in selling cattle and wood off the place, from which master had no benefit, in consequence of which, I was privately made a sort of watchman over the place.

After W—, the next overseer, was my master's brother. At the end of two years, they fell out about settling — the master said he was broke: they drew knives, threatening each other, but did not use them. Master said he would take the best slaves off the place, and then sell the place, with the sorriest ones on it. Then he said he couldn't pay his brother in money, but his brother might take it in slaves. The brother picked out myself, wife, and two children and two others, which was too many. Master objected — then they drew the knives. Master gave him me, wife, and children. At night, fearing he might take the others, he took them himself, to his upper place, where he lived above Natchez.

My new master removed us to Kentucky. We were all the slaves he had. We raised tobacco, oats, etc. I considered my treatment worse than at any other place. They gave me great encouragement to come with them, promising me well. Among other things, he promised to pay me $10.25, earned by me at overwork chopping. After I got to Kentucky, I wanted a hat. I went and picked one out, and told the shopman I'd get the money of my master. I sent his son in to ask for it. He sent me word that if I mentioned money again, or told any person that he owed it, he would give me *five hundred lashes!* A while after, I asked him to *give* me a little money. "What do you want of money?" "To buy me a hat." "Isn't that hat good enough?" "It don't turn the water, and I see the colored people wearing respectable hats, and I want one to wear to meeting." He said "go to such a place, get a wool hat, and have it charged to me." I went and got it, — it was a poor thing, and cost one dollar. I did what he wanted as well as I could, to avoid punishment. I staid with him three years.

One day he had ordered me to draw some water on a sled: then he called me into the field. I stooped down to unloose a chain, — he hurried up to me with an axe in his hand. He says, "When I want you for one thing, you are sure to do another." I answered, "I've got to work till I die, and had as lief work at one thing as another." He threatened me with the axe — I didn't dodge. Then he threatened me that he would give me the five hundred lashes before many days. I thought he might finally undertake it, and that I'd better be off. I received assistance from kind friends, and reached Canada without difficulty about five years ago. I have had a serious time in my life.

I felt so thankful on reaching a land of freedom, that I couldn't express myself. When I look back at what I endured, it seems as if I had entered a Paradise. I can here sing and pray with none to molest me. I am a member of the Baptist Church, and endeavor to live a Christian life.

I rent a piece of land, and make out to live. My family are sickly, so that I have not been able to purchase land. But I am not discouraged, and intend to work on while I have health and strength, and to live such a life as I should wish when I come to die.

17

Statements By and About Black Refugees in Canada

Tales of Slave Owners About Canada

The slaveholders sometimes tell the slaves stories about Canada to prevent their running away. I understood that Canada was 9000 miles off, & that it was so cold there that we couldn't do any thing.

— J.W. Lindsay[1]

I have heard it as common talk, that the wild geese were so common in Canada, that they would scratch a man's eyes out; that corn wouldn't grow there, nor any thing else but rice; that every thing they had there was imported.

— Dan Fackart[2]

After we began to hear about Canada, our master used to tell us all manner of stories about what a dreadful place it was; and we believed some of them, but some we didn't. When they told us that we must pay half of our wages to the Queen, every day, it didn't seem strange nor wrong; but when they said it was so cold there that men going mowing had to break the ice with their scythes, I didn't believe that, because it was onreasonable. I knew grass wouldn't grow where ice was all the time.

— J. Lindsey[3]

Racial Prejudice in the United States and Canada

I find more prejudice here than I did in York State. When I was at home, I could go anywhere; but here, my goodness: you get an insult on every side. But the colored people have their rights before the law; that is the only thing that has kept me here.

— Mrs. Brown[4]

I must say that, leaving the law out of the question, I find that prejudice here is equally strong as on the other side. The law is the only thing that sustains us in this country.

— G.F. Simpson[5]

Contrasting what I feel now and what I was in the south, I feel as if a weight were off me. Nothing would induce me to go back, — nothing would carry me back. I would rather be wholly poor and be free, than to have all I could wish and be a slave. I am now in a good situation and doing well, — I am learning to write.

— Henry Williamson[6]

Stay in Canada or Return to the United States?

If slavery remains just as it is, I will stay in Canada. I have no idea of going back unless freedom is established.

— Henry Stewart[7]

I like Canada. If the United States were as free as Canada, I would still prefer to live here. I can do as much toward a living here in three days, as there in six.

— William A. Hall[8]

If slavery were abolished, I would rather live in a southern State, — I would work for some one, but I should want to have a piece of land of my own.

— Isaac Williams[9]

17. Statements by and About Black Refugees in Canada

Segregated and Integrated Schools in Canada

It does not work well with us to have colored children in school with whites. In our community, there is more prejudice against the colored people, and the children receive it from their parents. The colored children must feel it, for the white children refuse to play with them in the playground.

—White Headmaster of London High School[10]

I had charge of the Provincial Model School at Toronto for over ten years, and I have had charge of this school for over four years, and have had colored children under my charge all that time. They conduct themselves with the strictest propriety, and I have never known as occasion where the white children have had any difficulty with them on account of color. At first, when any new ones came, *I used to go out with them in the playground myself, and play with them specifically,* just to show I made no distinction whatever; and then the children made none....

Little white children do not show the slightest repugnance in playing with the colored children, or coming in contact with them....but sometimes parents will not let their children sit at the same desk with a colored child....we have no difficulty. We give the children their seats according to their credit marks in the preceding month, and I never have had the slightest difficulty.

—White principal of the High School, Hamilton[11]

The Providence of God and Slaves in Canada

Canada was a sort of Land of Canaan to the Negro. He sang, sighed, and longed to get there.... In spite of its distance from the South, nothing but physical and brute force could prevent their striving to get there. What but the Providence of God can account for the fact that

Washington and his contemporaries did not extend their dominion farther north?[12]

— S.J. Celestine Edwards

Charity for Refugees

My wish to the people of the States is, to give no more money to the begging agencies. If they wish to give money to the fugitives and the sick, it should be given to the True Band societies, who can disburse it as it is wanted. The Band will attend to the fugitives.

— Robert Nelson[13]

The people have been told absolute falsehoods about our freezing and suffering, and money has been raised which does no good. It has been reported to us, that thousands of dollars have been raised for our benefit, of which we have never received the first red cent. I say so — I am fifty-five years old, and have ever tried to keep the truth on my side.

— Robert Martin[14]

Religion and Slave Ownership

Those who were Christians & held slaves were the hardest masters. A card-player and drunkard wouldn't flog you half to death. Well, it is something like this — the Christians will oppress you more. For instance, the biggest dinner must be got on Sunday. Now, everybody that has got common sense knows that Sunday is a day of rest. And if you do the least thing in the world that they don't like, they will mark it down against you, and Monday you have got to take a whipping. Now, the card-player & horse racer won't be there to trouble you. They will eat their breakfast in the morning and feed their dogs, & then be off & you won't see them again till night. I would rather be with a card player or sportsman, by half, than a Christian.

— Mrs. Joseph Smith[15]

17. Statements by and About Black Refugees in Canada

The man who brought me up was a Baptist preacher, and was a little more indulgent than some others.

— John Dunn[16]

I was owned by High Hosler, a hide sorter, a man said to be rich, a good Catholic, though very disagreeable; he was not cruel, but was very driving and abusive in his language towards colored people.

— Orlando J. Hunt[17]

A White Doctor on Illnesses of Blacks in Canada

I think the colored people stand the climate very badly. In a very short time lung disease is developed, and they go by phthisis. The majority do not pass forty years. Of course, there are exceptions. They die off fast. I suppose I have had thirty colored people here with little children, with scrofulous disease, extending as far as ulceration of the temporal bone. Then they are a good deal subject to rheumatism. They bear a great many children, but raise only about one-half of them, I think. The children are generally weakly and puny; not so strong as our white children. A great many of them die in childhood. The principal disease is tubercular deposition of the stomach and intestines.

— Dr. Fisher, physician at
the Provincial Lunatic Assylum[18]

An Escaped Slave Seeks Treatment in Amherstburg for Tuberculosis.

I have been cook for large hotels. My health is now very poor, — I have had a bad cough for two or three years, from overwork — cooking sometimes for three hundred persons in a hotel. I have always supported myself, and have some money by me yet. I reside in Chatham, and came here to see a physician.

— Charles Brown[19]

A Mob

Up at the oil springs, the colored people have quite a little town. The white people were there, and they had all the work. They charged six shillings for sawing a cord of wood. The colored people went up there from Chatham, and, in order to get constant employment, they charged only fifty cents a cord. What did the white people do? They raised a mob, went one night and burned every shanty that belonged to a colored person, and drove them off entirely. Well, it was a mob; it was not society at all; it was but the dregs of society who did this.... The parties were arrested, and two of them went to the penitentiary for seven years.

— Mr. McCullum, president teacher
of the Hamilton High School[20]

18

God Save Queen Victoria

    In the 1830s and 1840s, escaping slaves could begin new lives in Philadelphia, New York, Boston, New Bedford, and other cities and towns, and in the countryside above the Mason-Dixon Line, though they were in some danger from slave-catchers attempting to claim a bounty. The number of blacks going into Canada in those years was small, and those fugitives joined an even smaller number who had fled there before 1830 or had been freed by the British during the Revolutionary War and the War of 1812. With the passage of the Fugitive Slave Act of 1850, the number of slaves entering Canada — mostly into Canada West — increased dramatically, often helped along by black and white abolitionists.

    We have told the stories of several of these emigrants — some escaped slaves, some born free — and their travails in reaching Canada, their finding freedom (and prejudice) once they were on Canadian soil, and their later lives. Some, like the Rev. Josiah Henson, were exuberant as they recognized they could begin to control their own destinies once they reached Canada, and others were discouraged by the strong racial prejudices they found in their adopted country.

    Lewis C. Chalmers, interviewed in Canada in 1863, had this recollection. He went to a white church one Sunday.

    The sexton asked, "What do you want here to-day?"

    "Is there not to be service here to-day?"

    "Yes, but we don't want any niggers here."

    "You are mistaken in the man. I am not a 'nigger,' but a negro."[1]

    But blacks in Canada were able to stand up for their rights under

British law when they were discriminated against. They argued for desegregated schools, though they did not always prevail and large numbers of schools remained segregated. They could assert themselves as they certainly could not in the South. When black Alfred Shadd was in medical school at the University of Toronto, some white students did not want to sit with him. Sit with me or fight me, he declared. His fellow students sat with him.

The obstacles faces by blacks in their new country were formidable. As Benjamin Miller, who lived in London, Canada West, said in an interview published in 1855: "We that begin here illiterate men, have to go against wind and tide. We have a learned, enterprising people to contend with; we have a colder climate than we have been used to, to contend with; we have our own ignorance and poverty to contend with. It takes a smart man to do all that; but many do it, all make a living, and some do lay up money."[2]

Some blacks faced strong local prejudice with anger, though others had a pioneer spirit, worked around prejudice, and saw vast opportunities in their new country.

Most of the refugees came to Canada with few possessions and little or no funds. Black and white church groups and philanthropists gave support through Hiram Wilson and others who helped the new arrivals with clothes, gave information about housing and jobs, and often provided small sums while the refugees were getting established. Plans, often grandiose and without proper funding, were made for colonies for blacks, and except for Elgin, all failed. The smaller, personalized organizations such as the one administered by Hiram Wilson in St. Catharines (after he left Dawn), the Toronto Ladies' Association for the Relief of Destitute Colored Fugitives, and the all-black True Band found throughout Canada West were all successful. The True Band, striving for equal opportunities for blacks, agitated for better schools and gave financial help to new arrivals and to the sick and elderly. Proud people in the True Band were taking care of each other the best they could and with limited resources which they had not garnered by outside "begging."

We have included stories about blacks of high achievement such as several members of the Shadd family, of black doctors, of pioneer

18. God Save Queen Victoria

farmers, of successful business people, of a remarkable black Union army chaplain. We have the stories of two real people who figure in the composite portraits of Eliza Harris and Uncle Tom in Harriet Beecher Stowe's *Uncle Tom's Cabin*. We give an account of the rescued Shadrach's early failures to get a footing in Canada, followed by his modest success as a barber. Shadrach was one of the minority of blacks who did not return to the United States after the Civil War ended. The large Shadd family had some strong members who stayed in Canada and others who found success during Reconstruction in Washington, D.C., and in Mississippi.

Most of the refugees, however, were not remarkable for their successes or for their failures. Benjamin Miller, interviewed in 1863, understood: "I have done first rate here. I will tell you what I call first-rate, and then you can judge. I say first rate, from the fact that we have to row against wind and tide when we get here, and being brought up illiterate, I consider that if we live and keep our families well fed and clad, we have done first-rate."[3] Unfortunately, there were few interviews of those in the vast majority who could do no more than feed and clothe and house their families and get some schooling for their children. Their lives were better than they had been in slavery and better than they had been in the North, for they were more adequately protected by British law.

The supposedly unremarkable blacks in Canada were remarkable because they survived even though most were illiterate when they arrived; they were poor, and they were black in a country where many of the white citizens were overt or secret racists. Most left Canada after the end of the Civil War, for the pull of the United States was strong. They felt a new day was coming during Reconstruction, but we now know they were deceived, for most of their rights in the South, especially, were gone by 1900. Many did have the personal satisfaction, though, of being near friends and relatives once they left Canada.

What is implicit in the stories is the desire for freedom, pursued often with great personal risk and practiced in a new country with many racist citizens but with government officials who offered the protection of British law. In addition, some white ministers, teachers, newspaper editors, and women's groups, as well as black individuals and organizations, worked to aid refugee blacks in Canada.

Joseph Taper, a runaway slave living in St. Catharines, Canada West, wrote to a white acquaintance, Joseph Long of New Town, Virginia, on November 11, 1840, about his new life in Canada. With his family, Taper had followed the gou'd [gourd: the Big Dipper] to Canada in 1837 and had become a successful farmer. He requested that his letter be sent on to his former master, Bryan Martin Stevens. In the letter, Taper began with the theme of liberty:

"I now take this opportunity to inform you that I am in a land of liberty...." He continued, "Since I have been in the Queens dominions I have been well contented, Yes well contented for Sure, man is as God intended he should be. That is, all are born free & equal. This is a wholesome law, not like the Southern laws which puts man made in the image of God, on level with brutes." He described in detail his bountiful harvest of potatoes, corn, buckwheat, and his many farm animals. His son, not yet six years old, was already reading, and Taper wrote, "I intend keeping him in school until he becomes a good scholar." Taper ended his letter with a description of a domestic scene that had been made possible by the British government: "My wife and self are sitting by a good comfortable fire happy, knowing that there are none to molest or make us afraid. God save Queen Victoria. The Lord bless her in this life, & crown her with glory in the world to come in my prayer."[4] The Canadian light was keeping the Tapers and thousands of other blacks secure and unafraid, for their new government gave them rights denied to them in the United States.

Chapter Notes

Preface

1. Hill, *Call & Response*, 236, 238.
2. Drew, *The Refugee*, 211.

Chapter 1

1. We have made use of Winks, *Blacks in Canada* and Hill, *The Freedom-Seekers*. We recommend Winks for his discussion of blacks freed by the British for their service in the Revolutionary War and their resettlement in the Maritime Provinces of Canada, and Schama in *Rough Crossings* for his vivid accounts of these blacks, some of whom were later resettled in Sierra Leone. After 1830 or so, most blacks settled in Canada West (now Ontario), and most of our material concerns these settlers. Shadrach, who fled to Montreal, is an exception.
2. Hill, *Freedom-Seekers*, 3.
3. *Ibid.*
4. *Ibid.*, 4.
5. Winks, *Blacks in Canada*, 10.
6. Hill, *Freedom-Seekers*, 6.
7. James Oliver Horton and Lois E. Horton, *Slavery and the Making of America*, (New York: Oxford University Press, 2005).
8. Winks, *Blacks in Canada*, 24–60.
9. Hochschild, *Bury the Chains*, 48–51.
10. *Ibid.*, 50.
11. *Ibid.*
12. *Ibid.*, 50–51.
13. *Ibid.*, 81.
14. Rice, *Radical Narratives of the Black Atlantic*, 70.
15. Hochschild, *Bury the Chains*, 87.
16. *Ibid.*, 88–97, 111–116.
17. *Ibid.*, 153, 158–162, 168, 188, 230–234, 236, 252, 255, 346.
18. Hill, *Freedom-Seekers*, 14–18; Winks, *Blacks in Canada*, 96–99; Scott, *John Graves Simcoe* is useful for details.
19. Scott, *John Graves Simcoe*, 90.
20. Winks, *Blacks in Canada*, 96–99.
21. Hill, *Freedom-Seekers*, 15–19.
22. *Ibid.*, 93.
23. Frost, *I've Got a Home in Glory Land*, 193–225, has many specific examples.
24. Hill, *Freedom-Seekers*, 94–95.
25. Winks, *Blacks in Canada*, 179–180, 195–200.
26. *Ibid.*, 197–200.
27. Drew, *The Refugee*, 165–167.
28. Winks, *Blacks in Canada*, 256–257.
29. *Ibid.*, 178–232.
30. Pease and Pease, *Black Utopia*, 46–62; Winks, *Blacks in Canada*, 156–162; Hill, *Freedom-Seekers*, 67–71.
31. Pease and Pease, *Black Utopia*, 63–83; Winks, *Blacks in Canada*, 178–181; Hill, *Freedom-Seekers*, 71–74.
32. Pease and Pease, *Black Utopia*, 109–122; Winks, *Blacks in Canada*, 204–208; Hill, *Freedom-Seekers*, 74–76.
33. Pease and Pease, *Black Utopia*, 84–108; Winks, *Blacks in Canada*, 208–218; Hill, *Freedom-Seekers*, 76–89; Howe, *Refugees from Slavery*, 107–110.
34. Silverman, *Unwelcome Guests*, 157–158.
35. Howe, *Refugees from Slavery*, 76.
36. Winks, *Blacks in Canada*, 484–496.
37. Silverman, *Unwelcome Guests*, 159.

Chapter 2

1. Although it is possible that the owner changed the name Sherwood to Shadrach, it is much more likely that the religious young man chose a new name with its overtones of deliverance. If he had disliked the name of Shadrach, he would have changed it after he reached Boston and Montreal.
2. For an excellent account of Shadrach's early life, see Gary Collison, *Shadrach Minkins*, 1–38.
3. *Ibid.*, 39–57. Collison provides specific details of the escape.
4. *Ibid.*, 65–67. Collison gives many details about Shadrach's work at the coffee shop.
5. *Ibid.*, 82.
6. *Ibid.*, 110–115.
7. *Ibid.*, 118.
8. *Ibid.*, 91–165. Collison provides dramatic details about Shadrach's deliverance and escape to Montreal.
9. *Ibid.*, 169–216. Collison's findings on Shadrach's life in Montreal are especially commendable.

Chapter 3

1. Stowe, *Uncle Tom's Cabin*, 106.
2. Bordewich, *Bound for Canaan*, 370.
3. *Ibid.*, 370–373.
4. Stowe, *Uncle Tom's Cabin*, introduction by Darryl Pinckney, vii–xxii is perceptive on the structure of the novel.
5. We are using *Father Henson's Story of His Own Life*, (Boston: John P. Jewett and Company, 1858). See Winks, *Blacks in Canada*, 183–184, 191–195, for shrewd comments on the various editions of Henson's slave narrative.
6. Henson, *Father Henson's Story*, 6–7.
7. *Ibid.*, 8–15.
8. *Ibid.*, 31–37.
9. *Ibid.*, 38–40.
10. *Ibid.*, 40.
11. *Ibid.*, 41.
12. *Ibid.*, 45–47.
13. *Ibid.*, 51.
14. *Ibid.*, 55–59.
15. *Ibid.*, 60.
16. Stowe, *Uncle Tom's Cabin*, 45.
17. Henson, *Father Henson's Story*, 66–78.
18. *Ibid.*, 79–80.
19. *Ibid.*, 84–85.
20. *Ibid.*, 89–91.
21. Stowe, *Uncle Tom's Cabin*, 428–429.
22. Quoted in Hill, *Freedom-Seekers*, 227, note 7, second column.
23. Henson, *Father Henson's Story*, 97.
24. *Ibid.*, 99–101.
25. *Ibid.*, 104.
26. Blassingame, *Slave Testimony*, 153.
27. Henson, *Father Henson's Story*, 106.
28. *Ibid.*, 111.
29. *Ibid.*, 113–115.
30. *Ibid.*, 117–119.
31. *Ibid.*, 121–123.
32. *Ibid.*, 123.
33. *Ibid.*, 123–125.
34. *Ibid.*, 125.
35. *Ibid.*, 126.
36. *Ibid.*, 127.
37. *Ibid.*, 128–130.
38. *Ibid.*, 130.
39. *Ibid.*, 130–133.
40. *Ibid.*, 133–135.
41. *Ibid.*, 135.
42. *Ibid.*, 138–141.
43. *Ibid.*, 140–143.
44. *Ibid.*, 165–166.
45. Winks, *Blacks in Canada*, 195–196.
46. *Ibid.*, 179–180, 195–197; Hill, *Freedom-Seekers*, 71–72.
47. Winks, *Blacks in Canada*, 178–181, 195–204, on successes and failure of Dawn; Henson, *Father Henson's Story*, 165–172, has a bland account of Dawn; Pease and Pease, *Black Utopia*, 63–83; Hill, *Freedom-Seekers*, 71–74.
48. Winks, *Blacks in Canada*, 191–193.
49. *Ibid.*, 184–195.
50. Andrews, *To Tell a Free Story*, 119.
51. Stowe, *A Key to Uncle Tom's Cabin*, 22.
52. *Ibid.*, 21; Stowe, *Uncle Tom's Cabin*, 8.
53. Hagedorn, *Beyond the River*, 135–136.
54. *Ibid.*, 136–137.

55. *Ibid.*, 137.
56. *Ibid.*, 137–139.
57. *Ibid.*, 139.
58. Coffin, *Reminiscences*, 147–151; Hagedorn, *Beyond the River*, 139.
59. Hagedorn, *Beyond the River*, 300.
60. Stowe, *Uncle Tom's Cabin*, 86–98.
61. *Ibid.*, 101–103.
62. *Ibid.*, 146–156.
63. *Ibid.*, 206.
64. *Ibid.*, 215.
65. *Ibid.*, 220–221, 413–415.
66. *Ibid.*, 403.
67. *Ibid.*, 458–466.
68. *Ibid.*, 469.
69. Hagedorn, *Beyond the River*, 208–209.
70. *Ibid.*, 209–210.
71. *Ibid.*, 210–211.
72. *Ibid.*, 211.
73. *Ibid.*
74. *Ibid.*, 211–212.
75. *Ibid.*, 213
76. *Ibid.*
77. *Ibid.*
78. Coffin, *Reminiscences*, 147–151.
79. Henson, *An Autobiography of the Reverend Josiah Henson ("Uncle Tom")*, 114–116.
80. Blassingame, *Slave Testimony*, 151–164; *American National Biography*, 4: 978–980.
81. Stowe, *Key to Uncle Tom's Cabin*, 13–21.

Chapter 4

1. *The Liberator*, June 10, 1842, p. 1: see Hendrick and Hendrick, *The Creole Mutiny*, 14.
2. Hendrick and Hendrick, *The Creole Mutiny*, 23.
3. *Ibid.*, 26.
4. Still, *The Underground Rail-Road*, 64–65.
5. Hendrick and Hendrick, *The Creole Mutiny*, 27–28.
6. *Ibid.*, 28–29.
7. *Ibid.*, 30.
8. *Ibid.*, 38.
9. *Ibid.*, 11–12, 77–83.
10. *Ibid.*, 12.
11. *Ibid.*, 109–110. Many writers reacted to the story of Madison Washington and his wife. Some concocted a happy ending for the love story: Madison's wife, unbeknownst to him, was on the *Creole* also being shipped to New Orleans. In this romantic — and totally untrue — story, Madison and his wife were reunited after the mutiny was successful. In *The Creole Mutiny* we give an account of five writers who wrote about Washington and the mutiny, 121–152.

Chapter 5

1. General information about the Shadd family is from Hill, *Freedom-Seekers*, 202–205; Winks, *Blacks in Canada*, 225–226, 395–397; Bearden and Butler, *Shadd*; Rhodes, *Mary Ann Shadd Cary*; and Thomson, *Blacks in Deep Snow*.
2. Bearden and Butler, *Shadd*, 26; quoted in Andrews, *To Tell a Free Story*, 157.
3. Biographical information about Henry Bibb is from *American National Biography*, 2: 717–718; Hill, *Freedom-Seekers*, 155–156.
4. Hill, *Freedom-Seekers*, 147–161.
5. Bearden and Butler, *Shadd*, 34–42, 43–48, 69, 92.
6. *Ibid.*, 122. Jane Rhodes in *Mary Ann Shadd Cary* is insightful about Shadd and the Bibbs.
7. Winks, *Blacks in Canada*, 203, 206–207, 225–226, 261, 397.
8. *Ibid.*, 395.
9. Hill, *Freedom-Seekers*, 155–156.
10. Winks, *Blacks in Canada*, 261; Hill, *Freedom-Seekers*, 203.
11. Hill, *Freedom-Seekers*, 20–23.
12. *Ibid.*; see also Rhodes, *Mary Ann Shadd Cary* and Bearden and Butler, *Shadd*.
13. *American National Biography*, 6: 282–283; see also Rhodes, *Mary Ann Shadd Cary* and Bearden and Butler, *Shadd*.
14. The best accounts of Shadd's later years are Rhodes, *Mary Ann Shadd Cary* and Bearden and Butler, *Shadd*.
15. Sterling, in *The Trouble They Seen*, 151–152, gives an account of Shadds in Mississippi. For other accounts of Shadds see

Hill, *Freedom-Seekers*, 138–171, 202–205, 214.

16. *American National Biography*, 19: 697–698.

17. Hill, *Freedom-Seekers*, 202–205; Thomson, *Blacks in Deep Snow*, 44–49.

18. Thomson, *Blacks in Deep Snow*, 51.

19. *Ibid.*, 50, 55–56.

20. *Ibid.*, 53–54.

21. *Ibid.*, 52–53.

22. *Ibid.*, 53–54.

23. *Ibid.*, 55.

24. *Ibid.*, 58.

Chapter 6

1. The text of Richardson's speech, Bibb's reply, and the notes are in Blassingame, *Slave Testimony*, 164–165.

2. *Ibid.*, 164.

3. *Ibid.*

4. *Ibid.*, 165.

5. *Ibid.*

6. *Ibid.*, 166.

7. *Ibid.*

8. *Ibid.*

9. *Ibid.*

10. *Ibid.*, 164, note 17.

11. *Ibid.*, 165, note 19.

12. *Ibid.*, 164, note 18.

13. *Ibid.*

14. Frost, *I've Got a Home in Glory Land*, 205.

15. Remini, *Henry Clay*, 26–27; 73–74; 204; 205, note 41; 484, note 42; 619; 770.

Chapter 7

1. Karolyn Smardz Frost supervised the 1985 archaeological dig on the Blackburn's property in Toronto. She then began extensive historical research about Thornton Blackburn and his wife. Ms. Frost's book, *I've Got a Home in Glory Land: A Lost Tale of the Underground Railroad*, is a unique study, careful and revealing. We are greatly indebted to it. See page 28 for Blackburn's father.

2. Frost, *I've Got a Home in Glory Land*, 29–30.

3. *Ibid.*, 35–36.

4. *Ibid.*, 45.

5. *Ibid.*, 53–70.

6. *Ibid.*, 76–79.

7. *Ibid.*, 81–82.

8. *Ibid.*, 94–99.

9. Stowe, *Uncle Tom's Cabin*, 397.

10. Hendrick and Hendrick, *Creole Mutiny*, 42; Walter Johnson, *Soul by Soul*, 147–149.

11. Stowe, *Uncle Tom's Cabin*, 281, 290.

12. Hendrick and Hendrick, *Creole Mutiny*, 18–19; Still, *Underground Rail Road*, 81–86.

13. Hendrick and Hendrick, *Creole Mutiny*, 17–18.

14. Frost, *I've Got a Home in Glory Land*, fourth page of illustrations following 228.

15. *Ibid.*, 10–14.

16. *Ibid.*, 119, 120, 123–124, 150.

17. *Ibid.*, 160–165.

18. *Ibid.*, 163–190. Frost gives a dramatic account of the legal troubles of the Blackburns in Detroit.

19. *Ibid.*, 194, 201.

20. *Ibid.*, 254–269. An excellent account of the Blackburns in Toronto.

21. *Ibid.*, 280.

22. *Ibid.*, 287–288.

23. *Ibid.*, 338, 347–348.

Chapter 8

1. Hendrick and Hendrick, *Fleeing for Freedom*, 8. Henrietta Buckmaster, in *Let My People Go*, is insightful about the work of Thomas Garrett.

2. Buckmaster, *Let My People Go*, 151; Hendrick and Hendrick, *Fleeing for Freedom*.

3. Quoted in Hendrick and Hendrick, *Why Not Every Man?*, 108.

4. Still, *The Underground Rail Road*, 512.

5. *Ibid.*, 513.

6. *Ibid.*

7. *Ibid.*

8. *Ibid.*

9. *Ibid.*

10. *Ibid.*, 514.

11. Frost, *I've Got a Home in Glory Land*, 288, 301.
12. *Ibid.*, 302.
13. *Ibid.*
14. *Ibid.*, 334–335.
15. *Ibid.*, 285, 334.
16. Still, *The Underground Rail Road*, 513.

7. *Ibid.*, 435–436.
8. *Ibid.*, 440–441.
9. *Ibid.*, 441–442.
10. *Ibid.*, 444.
11. *Ibid.*
12. *Ibid.*, 445.
13. *Ibid.*, 446.

Chapter 9

1. Clinton, *Harriet Tubman*, 3–23; *American National Biography*, 21: 888–889; Blassingame, *Slave Testimony*, 457–458.
2. Clinton, *Tubman*, 29–30.
3. The *Freedmen's Record* interview is republished in Blassingame, *Slave Testimony*, 457–465. The quotation from the song is from p. 458.
4. Clinton, *Tubman*, 34.
5. *Ibid.*, 34–38, 46–60.
6. *Ibid.*, 79–81.
7. *Ibid.*, 84.
8. Blassingame, *Slave Testimony*, 461.
9. *Ibid.*, 459.
10. *Ibid.*, 462; Drew, *The Refugee*, 20; Still, *The Underground Rail Road*, 296–299; Clinton, *Tubman*, 86.
11. Blassingame, *Slave Testimony*, 462.
12. *Ibid.*, 460; Clinton, *Tubman*, 83.
13. Drew, *The Refugee*, 20.
14. Clinton, *Tubman*, 112–115.
15. *Ibid.*, 115–116.
16. *Ibid.*, 117.
17. *Ibid.*, 191–214.

Chapter 10

1. Coffin, *Reminiscences*, (1876), 428–446; Hendrick and Hendrick reproduce the chapter in *Fleeing for Freedom*, 78–90. All references are to the 1876 edition. Hagedorn, author of the admirable *Beyond the River*, is conducting research on Fairfield, see 309–310.
2. Coffin, *Reminiscences*, 429.
3. *Ibid.*, 430.
4. *Ibid.*, 430–431.
5. *Ibid.*, 431–432.
6. *Ibid.*, 432.

Chapter 11

1. Quoted in Glatthaar, *Forged in Battle*, xiii.
2. Miller, "Garland H. White," 203.
3. Miller, "Garland H. White," 203; for a sketch of Toombs, *American national Biography*, 21: 729–730.
4. Miller, "Garland H. White," 203.
5. *Ibid.*, 204.
6. *Ibid.*
7. Drew, *The Refugee*, 103.
8. Miller, "Garland H. White," 203.
9. *Ibid.*, 204.
10. *Ibid.*, 205.
11. *Ibid.*, 206.
12. *Ibid.*, 207.
13. *Ibid.*, 208.
14. *Ibid.*, 208–210; Redkey, *Grand Army of Black Men*, 110–113; Trudeau, *Like Men of War*, 228–251; Glatthaar, *Forged in Battle*, 150–151; Hine, Hine, and Harrold, *The African-American Odyssey*, 245–246.
15. Redkey, *A Grand Army of Black Men*, 111.
16. Miller, "Garland H. White," 209.
17. Redkey, *A Grand Army of Black Men*, 111.
18. Miller, "Garland H. White," 211.
19. *Ibid.*, 210–211.
20. Redkey, *A Grand Army of Black Men*, 176.
21. *Ibid.*, 176–177.
22. *Ibid.*, 178.
23. *Ibid.*, 133–134.
24. *Ibid.*, 134.
25. *Ibid.*, 135–136.
26. *Ibid.*, 136.
27. *Ibid.*, 201–202.
28. *Ibid.*, 202.
29. *Ibid.*

30. Miller, "Garland H. White," 214.
31. *Ibid.*, 216–218.

Chapter 12

1. *American National Biography*, 1: 252–254.
2. Hill, *The Freedom-Seekers*, 169.
3. *Ibid.*, 168.
4. *American National Biography*, 1: 752–753.
5. *Ibid.*, 1: 753.
6. Tobin, *From Midnight to Dawn*, 231.
7. *American National Biography*, 1: 753.
8. Glatthaar, *Forged in Battle*, 197.
9. *Ibid.*
10. *American National Biography*, 1: 753.
11. *Ibid.*
12. *Ibid.*

Chapter 13

1. Hill, *The Freedom-Seekers*, 205–206.
2. *Ibid.*, 206; Winks, *Blacks in Canada*, 328.
3. Hill, *The Freedom-Seekers*, 206; Winks, *Blacks in Canada*, 329.
4. Hill, *The Freedom-Seekers*, 206–208; Winks, *Blacks in Canada*, 329–330; *American National Biography*, 1: 15–16; Tobin, *From Midnight to Dawn*, 229–232.
5. *American National Biography*, 1: 15.
6. *Ibid.*
7. Tobin, *From Midnight to Dawn*, 231–232.
8. *Ibid.*
9. *American National Biography*, 1: 15.
10. http://providentfoundation.org/history.1.htm.
11. *American National Biography*, 1: 15.

Chapter 14

1. Still, *The Underground Rail Road*, 191.
2. *Ibid.*
3. *Ibid.*
4. *Ibid.*
5. *Ibid.*, 192.
6. *Ibid.*, 193; the dialogue is based on Hill's second letter from Canada.
7. *Ibid.*
8. *Ibid.*
9. *Ibid.*, 195.
10. *Ibid.*, 195–196.
11. *Ibid.*, 197.
12. Still gives accounts of the escapes of Hezekiah and James Hill, 200–203.
13. Howe, *Refugees from Slavery*, 73–75.
14. *Ibid.*, 73.
15. *Ibid.*, 75.
16. *Ibid.*, 74.
17. *Ibid.*
18. Still, *The Underground Rail Road*, 203.

Chapter 15

1. Drew, *The Refugee*, 139.
2. *Ibid.*, 141.
3. *Ibid.*, 139–140.
4. *Ibid.*, 140.
5. *Ibid.*
6. Thoreau, "Civil Disobedience," original title "Resistance to Civil Government," 1754.
7. Douglass, *The Narratives*, 68.
8. Drew, *The Refugee*, 141.
9. *Ibid.*
10. *Ibid.*, 142.
11. *Ibid.*
12. *Ibid.*
13. *Ibid.*, 142–143.
14. *Ibid.*, 143.
15. Douglass, *The Narratives*, 75–81.
16. Drew, *The Refugee*, 144.
17. *Ibid.*
18. *Ibid.*, 157–158.
19. *Ibid.*, 147–148, 158–159.
20. *Ibid.*, 148, 159.
21. Jacobs, *Incidents in the Life of a Slave Girl*, 19.
22. Drew, *The Refugee*, 148–149, 159.
23. *Ibid.*, 149.
24. Hendrick and Hendrick, *Two Slave Rebellions at Sea*, 31.
25. Drew, *The Refugee*, 149–150.
26. *Ibid.*, 151, 159.
27. *Ibid.*, 161.
28. *Ibid.*, 162.
29. *Ibid.*

30. *Ibid.*
31. *Ibid.*
32. *Ibid.*, 151.
33. *Ibid.*, 152.
34. *Ibid.*
35. *Ibid.*, 153.
36. *Ibid.*, 152–154.
37. *Ibid.*, 152.
38. *Ibid.*, 154.
39. *Ibid.*
40. *Ibid.*, 163.
41. *Ibid.*
42. *Ibid.*, 156.
43. *Ibid.*, 153.

Chapter 17

1. Blassingame, *Slave Testimony*, 401.
2. Howe, *Refugees from Slavery*, 11.
3. *Ibid.* Linsay and Lindsey are apparently the same person.
4. Howe, *Refugees from Slavery*, 45.
5. *Ibid.*
6. Drew, *The Refugee*, 94.
7. Blassingame, *Slave Testimony*, 416.
8. Drew, *The Refugee*, 224.
9. *Ibid.*, 46.
10. Howe, *Refugees from Slavery*, 47–48.
11. *Ibid.*, 47.
12. Quoted in Frost, *I've Got a Home in Glory Land*, 221.
13. Drew, *The Refugee*, 261–162.
14. *Ibid.*, 236.
15. Blassingame, *Slave Testimony*, 411.
16. *Ibid.*, 438.
17. Still, *The Underground Rail Road*, 461.
18. Howe, *Refugees from Slavery*, 22.
19. Drew, *The Refugee*, 247.
20. Howe, *Refugees from Slavery*, 43.

Chapter 18

1. Blassingame, *Slave Testimony*, 413.
2. Drew, *The Refugee*, 131–132.
3. Blassingame, *Slave Testimony*, 439.
4. Franklin and Schweninger, *Runaway Slaves*, 324–325.

Bibliography

American National Biography. Oxford: Oxford University Press, 1999. 24 volumes plus supplement.

Andrews, William L. *To Tell a Free Story: The First Century of Afro-American Autobiography, 1760–1865.* Urbana: University of Illinois Press, 1986.

Bearden, Jim and Linda Jean Butler. *Shadd: The Life and Times of Mary Ann Shadd Cary.* Toronto: NC Press, Ltd., 1977.

Blassingame, John W. *Slave Testimony: Two Centuries of Letters, Speeches, Interviews, and Autobiographies.* Baton Rouge: Louisiana State University Press, 1977.

Bordewich, Fergus M. *The Underground Railroad and the War for the Soul of America.* New York: Amistad, 2005.

Breyfogle, William. *Make Free: The Story of the Underground Railroad.* Philadelphia: J.B. Lippincott, 1958.

Buckmaster, Henrietta. *Let My People Go: The Story of the Underground Railroad and the Growth of the Abolition Movement.* New York: Harper & Brothers, 1941. Reprinted by the University of South Carolina Press, 1992.

Clarke, Lewis, and Milton Clarke. *Narratives of the Sufferings of Lewis and Milton Clarke.* Boston: Bela Marsh, 1846. Reprinted by Arno Press & the *New York Times*, 1969.

Clinton, Catherine. *Harriet Tubman: The Road to Freedom.* Boston: Little, Brown, 2004.

Coffin, Levi. *Reminiscences.* Cincinnati: Western Tract Society, 1876. Reprinted by Augustus M. Kelly, Publishers, New York, 1968.

Collison, Gary. *Shadrach Minkins: From Fugitive Slave to Citizen.* Cambridge: Harvard University Press, 1997.

Douglass, Frederick. *The Narrative and Selected Writings.* New York: Modern Library, 1984.

Drew, Benjamin. *The Refugee: A North-Side View of Slavery.* Boston: Benjamin P. Jewett, 1856. Reprinted by Addison Wesley, Reading, MA, 1969.

Franklin, John Hope, and Loren Schweninger. *Runaway Slaves: Rebels on the Plantation.* New York: Oxford University Press, 1999.

Frost, Karolyn Smardz. *I've Got a Home in Glory Land: A Lost Tale of the Underground Railroad.* New York: Farrar, Straus and Giroux, 2007.

Fryer, Mary Beacock, and Christopher Draycott. *John Graves Simcoe, 1752–1806. A Biography.* Toronto: Dundurn, 1998.

Bibliography

Gara, Larry. *The Liberty Line: The Legend of the Underground Railroad.* Lexington: University of Kentucky Press, 1967.

Glatthaar, Joseph T. *Forged in Battle: The Civil War Alliance of Black Soldiers and White Officers.* New York: The Free Press, 1990.

Hagedorn, Ann. *Beyond the River: The Untold Story of the Heroes of the Underground Railroad.* New York: Simon & Schuster, 2002.

Hendrick, George, and Willene Hendrick. *The Creole Mutiny: A Tale of Revolt Aboard A Slave Ship.* Chicago: Ivan R. Dee, 2003.

_____, eds. *Fleeing for Freedom: Stories of the Underground Railroad as Told by Levi Coffin and William Still.* Chicago: Ivan R. Dee, 2004.

_____, eds. *Two Slave Rebellions at Sea.* St. James, NY: Brandywine Press, 2000.

_____. *Why Not Every Man? African Americans and Civil Disobedience in the Quest for the Dream.* Chicago: Ivan R. Dee, 2005.

Henson, Josiah. *An Autobiography of the Reverend Josiah Henson ("Uncle Tom").* London, Ontario: Schuyler, Smith, 1881. Reprinted by Addison-Wesley in 1969.

_____. *Father Henson's Story of His Own Life.* Boston: John P. Jewett, 1858. Reprinted by Corinth, New York, 1962.

Hill, Daniel. *The Freedom-Seekers: Blacks in Early Canada.* Agincourt, Canada: The Book Society of Canada, 1981.

Hill, Patricia Liggins. *Call & Response: The Riverside Anthology of the African American Literary Tradition.* Boston: Houghton Mifflin Company, 1998.

Hine, Darlene Clark, William C. Hine, And Stanley Harrold. *The African-American Odyssey.* Upper Saddle River, NJ: Prentice Hall, 2000.

Hochschild, Adam. *Bury the Chains: Prophets and Rebels in the Fight to Free an Empire's Slaves.* Boston: Houghton Mifflin, 2005.

Horton, James Oliver, and Lois E. Horton. *Slavery and the Making of America.* New York: Oxford University Press, 2005.

Howe, S.G. *The Refugees from Slavery in Canada West. Report to the Freedmen's Inquiry Commission.* Boston: Wright & Potter, Printers, 1864. Reprinted by Arno Press and the *New York Times*, 1969.

Jacobs, Harriet A. *Incidents in the Life of a Slave Girl,* ed. By George Hendrick and Willene Hendrick. St. James, NY: Brandywine Press, 1999.

Miller, Edward A., Jr. "Garland H. White, Black Army Chaplain." *Civil War History*, 43: 201–218.

Pease, William H., and Jane H. Pease. *Black Utopia: Negro Communal Experiments in America.* Madison: The State Historical Society of Wisconsin, 1963.

Redkey, Edwin S., ed. *A Grand Army of Black Men: Letters from African-American Soldiers in the Union Army, 1861–1865.* Cambridge: Cambridge University Press, 1992.

Remini, Robert W. *Henry Clay: Statesman for the Union.* New York: W.W. Norton, 1991.

Rhodes, Jane. *Mary Ann Shadd Cary: The Black Press and Protest in the Nineteenth Century.* Bloomington: Indiana University Press, 1998.

Rice, Alan. *Radical Narratives of the Black Atlantic.* New York: Continuum, 2003.

Schama, Simon. *Rough Crossings: Britain, the Slaves, and the American Revolution.* New York: HarperCollins, 2006.

Bibliography

Scott, Duncan Campbell. *John Graves Simcoe.* Toronto: Morang & Co., 1906.

Siebert, Wilbur H. *The Underground Railroad from Slavery to Freedom.* New York: Macmillan, 1898. Reprinted: New York: Russell & Russell, 1967.

Silverman, Jason H. *Unwelcome Guests: Canada West's Response to American Fugitive Slaves, 1800–1865.* New York: Associated Faculty Press, 1985.

Sterling, Dorothy, ed. *The Trouble They Seen: Black People Tell the Story of Reconstruction.* Garden City, NY: Doubleday, 1976.

Still, William. *The Underground Rail Road.* Philadelphia: Porter & Coates, 1872. Reprinted by Arno Press and the *New York Times*, 1968.

Stowe, Harriet Beecher. *A Key to Uncle Tom's Cabin.* Boston: John P. Jewett, 1853. Reprinted, Bedford, MA: Applewood, 1998.

_____. *Uncle Tom's Cabin.* Introduction by Darryl Pinckney. New York: Signet Classic, 1998.

Thomson, Colin A. *Blacks in Deep Snow: Black Pioneers in Canada.* Don Mills, Ontario, Canada: J.M. Dent & Sons, 1979.

Thoreau, Henry David. "Resistance to Civil Government," also known as "Civil Disobedience." New York: *The Norton Anthology of American Literature*, 1998. I; 1752–1767.

Tobin, Jacqueline L. *From Midnight to Dawn: The Last Tracks of the Underground Railroad.* New York: Doubleday, 2007.

Trudeau, Noah Andre. *Like Men of War: Black Troops in the Civil War 1862–1865.* New York: Little Brown, 1998.

Winks, Robin W. *The Blacks in Canada: A History*, 2nd. ed. Montreal & Kingston: McGill-Queens University Press, 1997.

Index

Abbott, Dr. Anderson Ruffin 107, 109, 111–112
Abbott, Wilson Ruffin 110–111
African Methodist Episcopal (AME) Church 28, 62, 97–98, 100
American Missionary Association 62, 64
Amherst, Jeffrey 5
Amherstburg, Canada 73, 75, 131–132
Anderson, Osborne P. 65
Andrews, William 43
Anti-Slavery Bugle 74
Anti-Slavery Society of Canada 13, 82, 86, 87
Artis, Eli 149
Augusta, Dr. A.T. 107–109, 111–112
Averill, Capt. 17–18

Barnett, Ambrose 75
"Battle of the Crater" 100–101
Beyond the River (Hagedorn) 1, 51
Bibb, Henry 16, 17, 60, 61, 63, 64, 65, 74
Bibb, Mary Miles 61, 62
Bigelow, Mr. and Mrs. Edwin 20
Bird, Mrs. 46
Bird, Senator 46
Blackburn, Ruthie (later Lucie) 78–83, 86–87
Blackburn, Thornton 77–83, 86–87
Blacks in Canada (Winks) 1
Blassingame, John 1
Bordewich, Fergus M. 1
Bound for Canaan (Bordewich) 1
Bowley, John 89
Bowley, Kaziah 89
Braddock, Gen. Edward 59
Brown, Charles 132–133, 161
Brown, George 18, 87
Brown, Henry "Box" 78
Brown, John 65, 66
Brown, Mrs. 158
Brown, William Wells 66

Burgoin, Mary O. 107
Burns, Anthony 132
Bury the Chains (Hochschild) 1, 9

Cadillac, Antoinne de la Mothe 4
Caphart, John 20
Cary, Linton 65, 67
Cary, Mary Ann Shadd *see* Shadd, Mary Ann
Cary, Sarah 65, 67
Cary, Thomas 65
Casey, Ephraim 149
Cassy 30–31, 48, 78
Chalmers, Lewis C. 163
Chapman, John 151
Chatham, Canada 45, 52
Christian Recorder 101
"Civil Disobedience" (Thoreau) 120
Clarke, Lewis G. 53
Clarkson, Thomas 8–9
Clay, Sen. Henry 73–76
Coffin, Catharine 52–53
Coffin, Levi 2, 45, 46, 52–53, 92–96
Colchester, Canada 143–145
Collins, Thomas 49, 50, 51
Compromise of 1850 19, 20
Cooley, Chloe 10
Couillard, Guillaume 3
Covey, Edward 120, 122
Craft, Ellen 79
Craft, William 79
Creole 55–58
The Creole Mystery (Hendrick and Hendrick) 57
Cronyn, Dr. 108

Daddy Walker 81
Davis, Thomas 49, 50, 51
Dawn 13, 15, 41, 164
Delany, Dr. Martin 65–66
Douglass, Frederick 20, 53, 54, 55, 120, 122, 124

Index

Dred Scott Decision 84
Drew, Benjamin 1, 91, 119, 127, 128, 129, 130–131
Dunmore, Lord 5
Dunn, John 161

Elgin Settlement 16, 17, 164
Eliot, Samuel A. 42
Emerson, Ralph Waldo 115

Fairfield, John 2, 92–96
Fisher, Dr. 161
Fletcher, Phineas 47
Flint, Dr. 124
Forman, Isaac 55
Free People of Color 59
Freedman's Record 89, 90
Freedom-Seekers (Hill) 1, 73
Freemen's Hospital 109, 111
French, Mrs. 81
Friend of Man 54, 56
From Midnight to Dawn (Tobin) 1
Frost, Karolyn Smardz 1, 83
Fugitive Slave Act 19–20, 60, 89, 91, 97, 134, 163

Garnet, Henry Highland 55
Garrett, Thomas 84–85, 91
Garrison, William Lloyd 59
Gifford, Zephaniah C. 56, 57
Gosfield, Canada 151
Grant, Ulysses S. 103
Grier, David 147–148

Hagedorn, Ann 1, 51
Hall, William A. 158
Halliday, Rachel 46–47
Halliday, Simeon 46–47
Hammond, Surgeon General 108
Happy, Jesse 12
Harris, Eliza 24, 30, 43–53, 165
Harris, George 47, 48, 53
Harris, Harry 44–47
Harris, Mr. 47
Hatfield, John 141–143
Hayden, Lewis 20
Head, Sir Francis Bond 12
Henning, Thomas 86
Henry V (Shakespeare) 101
Henson, Josiah 13, 15, 24–43, 53, 163, 165
Henson, Tom 38–39
The Heroic Slave (Douglass) 54, 124–125
Hibbard, Mr. and Mrs. 38
Hill, Daniel G. 1, 73
Hill, Hezekiah 116

Hill, James 116
Hill, John Henry 113–118
Hochschild, Adam 1, 9
Howe, S.G. 1, 116–118
Hughes, William 122
Hunt, Orlando J. 161

Incidents in the Life of a Slave Girl (Jacobs) 116
I've Got a Home in Glory Land (Frost) 1, 83

Jackson, Albert 87
Jackson, Ann Maria 82, 84–87
Jackson, Elizabeth (daughter) 59
Jackson, Elizabeth (mother) 59
Jackson, James Henry 86, 87
Jackson, Richard 87
Jacobs, Harriet 116, 124
Johnson, Andrew 104–105
Johnson, Thomas 151–156

Key to Uncle Tom's Cabin (Stowe) 42
King, Dr. Martin Luther, Jr. 105
King, Rev. William 16
Kirke, David 3
Koch, Dr. Robert 68

Lee, Robert E. 102
Legree, Simon 30–31, 78
LeJeune, Olivier 3
Liberator 54
Lightfoot, Mrs. 81
Lincoln, Abraham 98, 102, 103, 107, 111–112
Lincoln, Mary Todd 111–112
Lincoln, Robert 111
Lindsay, Dido Elizabeth 6
Lindsay (Lindsey), J.W. 157
Little, Mr. and Mrs. John 119–129
Litton, Bryce 26, 27
Lobb, John 42, 53
Loker, Tom 48
Long, Joseph 166
Louis XIV (king of France) 3–4
Lyons, William 138

Maitland, Sir Peregrine 11
Mansfield, Lord 6–7
Mapp, Samuel 103–104
Martin, Robert 160
McCague, Thomas 51
McCague, Mrs. Thomas 51
McCargo, Thomas 56
McCullum, Mr. 162
McKim, James 84
Merritt, William 56, 57

180

Index

Miller, Benjamin 164–165
Minkins, Eda 21
Minkins, Mary 21
Minkins, Shadrach 19–22, 23, 165
Minkins, William 21
Mitchell, John 113
Moore, Lindley Murray 55
Morris, Elijah 56–57
Moseby (Mosely) 11–12

Nelson, Robert 145–147
Nova Scotia 5–6

Osgoode, William 11

Panis (Indians) 4, 5
Parnell, Harriet 59
Peckard, Rev. Peter 8
Phillips, James 8
The Provincial Freeman 64, 65
Purvis, Robert 55

Quakers 6–8, 32, 45, 46, 47, 48, 55, 84, 92–96

Rankin, Calvin 45
Rankin, John 44–45, 46, 48–52, 94
Rankin, John (son) 45, 49, 51
Rankin, Mrs. John 44–45, 48
Rankin, Samuel 49
The Refugee: A North-Side View of Slavery (Drew) 1, 91, 119, 127, 128, 130–131
Refugee Home Society 16, 62–63
Refugee Slaves' Friend Society 14
Refugees from Slavery in Canada West (Howe) 1, 116–118
Reynolds, Emma 112
Rice, Isaac 13
Richardson, Lewis 73–76, 128
Riley, Amos 28–30, 32
Riley, Amos (son) 30–32
Riley, Isaac 25–28
Riley, Mrs. Isaac 2
Riseley, Mr. 40
Rogers, Thomas 80
Ross, Araminta *see* Tubman, Harriet
Rough Crossings (Schama) 1
Russell, Charles S. 99–101, 103–104
Ruth, Rev. William 150–151

St. Catharines, Canada 42, 164, 166
Sanford, Joseph 138–141
Schama, Simon 1
Seward, William Henry 91, 99
Shadd (Schad, Schadd, Shad), Abraham D. 59, 60, 63, 67, 68

Shadd (Schad, Schadd, Shad), Abraham W. 66
Shadd (Schad, Schadd, Shad), Absalom 65, 67
Shadd (Schad, Schadd, Shad), Dr Alfred Schmitz 68–72, 164
Shadd (Schad, Schadd, Shad), Amelia 59
Shadd (Schad, Schadd, Shad), Dr. Furman Jeremiah 67–68, 72
Shadd (Schad, Schadd, Shad), Garrison 67, 68
Shadd (Schad, Schadd, Shad), Hans 59, 72
Shadd (Schad, Schadd, Shad), Isaac 60, 64, 65, 67
Shadd (Schad, Schadd, Shad), Jeremiah 59
Shadd (Schad, Schadd, Shad), Mary Ann 16, 60–67, 98
Shadd (Schad, Schadd, Shad) Family 59–72, 164–165
Shadrach *see* Minkins, Shadrach
Shakespeare, William 101
Siebert, Wilbur H. 1, 119
Silverman, Jason H. 16–17
Simcoe, John Graves 9–11
Simpson, G.F. 158
Slaughter, James 80
Slave Testimony (Blassingame) 1
"Sleepy Polly" 81
Smith, James 133–134
Smith, Mrs. Joseph 160
Smith, Mr. and Mrs. 125–126
Society of Friends *see* Quakers
Somerset, James 6
Stanton, Edwin M. 98–99, 107
Stewart, Charles 6
Stewart, Henry 158
Still, William 1, 55, 84–85, 87, 88, 113, 118
Stowe, Harriet Beecher 23, 29, 30, 31, 42, 43, 45, 46, 47, 165

Taney, Chief Justice Roger 84
Taper, Joseph 166
Thoreau, Henry David 120
To Tell a Free Story (Andrews) 43
Tobin, Jaqueline L. 1
Toombs, Robert 97–100, 102
Toronto Ladies' Association for the Relief of Destitute Colored Fugitives 13, 164
Toyer, Ellen 110–111
Troy, Rev. William 135–138
True Band 13, 144, 160, 164
Tubman, Harriet 50, 88–91
Turner, J.M.W. 7

Uncle Tom's Cabin (Stowe) 23–24, 29, 30, 43–53, 78, 165

Index

The Underground Rail-Road (Still) 1
The Underground Railroad from Slavery to Freedom (Siebert) 1
Unwelcome Guests (Silverman) 16–17

Van Trompe, John 46
Victoria, Queen 43, 166
Vigilance Committee of Philadelphia 84–85, 114
Virchow, Dr. Rudolph 67–68
A Voice from Harpers Ferry (Anderson) 65
The Voice of the Fugitive 61, 64
Vrooman, William 10–11

Warren, Colonel 37
Washington, Madison 54–58

Waterford, Ephriam 148
White, Chap. Garland H. 97–106
Wilberforce, William 8–9
Wilberforce Colony 15
Williams, Dr. Daniel Hale 112
Williams, Isaac 158
Williamson, Henry 158
Willis, Mrs. 13, 82, 86
Wilson, Sen. Henry 109
Wilson, Hiram 12–13, 14, 15, 41, 54, 86, 91, 164
Wilson, Sheriff 81
Winks, Robin 1

Zong 7–8

www.ingramcontent.com/pod-product-compliance
Ingram Content Group UK Ltd.
Pitfield, Milton Keynes, MK11 3LW, UK
UKHW042013140426
5217IPUK00015B/1149